MY CAPTAIN AMERICA

*A Granddaughter's Memoir
of a Legendary Comic Book Artist*

Megan Margulies

PEGASUS BOOKS
NEW YORK LONDON

My Captain America

Pegasus Books, Ltd.
148 West 37th Street, 13th FL
New York, NY 10018

First Pegasus Books hardcover edition August 2020

Interior design by Sabrina Plomitallo-González, Pegasus Books

ISBN: 978-1-64313-464-2

10 9 8 7 6 5 4 3 2 1

Printed in the United States of America
Distributed by Simon & Schuster

To my girls, Lila and Edie.
May you always have the courage to make art of your own.

And, of course, this is for Daddy Joe.

The stories in this book were unearthed from my own memories, home videos, as well as from my grandfather's books, *My Life in Comics* and *The Comic Book Makers*. Fragments of this story were featured in essays in the *Washington Post* and *Woman's Day*. There are a few names that have been changed to protect the privacy of individuals.

Prologue

He lived in midtown Manhattan, forty blocks south of my family's apartment. A smile and nod to the doorman, up the elevator, and down to the end of the popcorn-walled hallway brought you to apartment 6M. "M for 'moron,'" he used to say.

As a child, I loved without questioning. I probably loved without knowing it. Since I was very young, my love blazed a bright path toward my grandfather—or, as I called him once I could talk, Daddy Joe. He created Captain America, the Fly, Fighting American, *Sick* magazine, and romance comics, among others. Most people remember him as a true comics legend. To me, Joe Simon was the man who loved to have a cigar every night, a fan blowing the smoke over a drawing table spattered with ink and paint and out his studio apartment window.

Even before my family's apartment became too much to bear, he was a calming force amid a city of millions. Out on the streets there were constant obstacles to maneuver around—people, construction, cars, wailing sirens—and places that were off-limits. *Don't go too far, don't run down the subway steps without me, don't touch those crack vials, watch out for that man, don't step on that lady.* And even inside the apartment I had parents to contend with—*don't eat that, don't leave your toys there, don't talk to the kids outside your window, don't forget to lock the door, stay out of my way.*

In Daddy Joe's apartment, I was on vacation from it all. His linen closet was stocked with the root beer I was forbidden from having at home; microwavable dinners were stacked in his freezer; and takeout menus for dozens of restaurants were scattered on his kitchen table. The view from his studio apartment was a partial downtown view, lights and dark windows—the simple version of New York. When I was with him, I loved the city. I saw the magic of it.

For a better view, we went up to the roof of his building. "Let's bring the camera," he suggested more than once.

The elevator climbed, skipping over the thirteenth floor, shaking enough to make me tense and look to Daddy Joe for reassurance. Once we were on the twenty-third floor and out of the elevator, there was a steep climb in the stairwell, the gray concrete steps echoing our stomps against the walls. With a hard shove, sometimes with my hip, the roof door flung open, getting caught in the wind and slamming against the side of the building—daylight almost knocking us off our feet.

Sometimes we separated immediately, Daddy Joe snapping photos of the skyline with his old Nikon, the photos to be used as inspiration for superheroes leaping over city buildings. I tried to make out figures in the windows across the way. Taller buildings blocked all of Central Park and uptown, where my family's apartment was.

"Careful!" he yelled in my direction as I gripped the metal railing and peered over the edge at the tiny cars and people below. He stood on the gravel, his eyes squinting behind his large-framed glasses, his long legs making him seem as tall as the surrounding buildings. "Come over here and let me take a photo of you."

Other times we stood together, looking west toward the Hudson River, catching a glimpse of New Jersey. The city buzzing, honking below us—the wind whipping my hair and dancing around our two bodies. I like to think that in these moments we were both happy—pretending to fly over the city like a superhero and the girl he rescued.

ONE

It All Began in New York

1913 and 1981

X

D addy Joe once told me that he came close to never being born. "My mother tried to get rid of me," he said with a laugh.

My great-grandmother Rose found out that she was pregnant only nine months after having my great-aunt Beatrice. Working as a button-maker, while my great-grandfather Harry worked as a tailor, Rose didn't believe they could afford another child. She begged her cousin Izzy, a pharmacist, to help with her predicament. He placed a pill in her palm and sent her on her way. Rose swallowed the aspirin, relieved to have her problem solved.

Daddy Joe was born on October 11, 1913.

He grew up in Rochester, New York. His father, Harry, came from Leeds, England, on the other side of the Atlantic. He had a lot of family in Rochester, one of them a cousin named Hymie. Hymie was tall and handsome, a lady's man. Harry wrote "Hymie Simon" on Daddy Joe's birth certificate without Rose knowing—she couldn't read English, only her native Russian and Yiddish. But when she found out, she was furious. She wanted Daddy Joe to be named Joseph, after her brother. Even though she got her way, his birth certificate was never changed. He was always legally—secretly—Hymie.

They called their apartment a "flat." It was railroad style, moving from front to back. The front of the apartment served as Harry's tailor shop, with windows only in a few rooms. On Sundays, after Rose and Harry were done with the newspaper, they handed over the comic strips to Daddy Joe and his sister, Beatrice. The two of them laid out the pages on the floor of the apartment's front room where, because it was used as Harry's shop, they enjoyed the modern luxury of electric lights.

Rochester was a city of manufacturers, including Eastman Kodak, the photography company, and Bausch + Lomb, the optical conglomerate. In an effort to contribute income to the family, a fourteen-year-old Daddy Joe sold newspapers on street corners, in front of the Kodak building, and in the Bausch + Lomb lobby for two cents each. Years later, he used his experience as a paperboy to create the *Newsboy Legion* for DC Comics, about a group of orphans living on the streets of Suicide Slum in New York City.

As a child, Daddy Joe knew only Rochester but saw many other places in the movies, including Broadway and the Big Apple. He dreamed of moving to New York City from a young age, but after high school, he stayed in Rochester, illustrating for the local newspaper and saving his money.

In 1937, at twenty-three years old and with a fine suit (thanks to his father), he set out toward his future in the big city. I like to imagine Daddy Joe walking the city streets, all legs and ambition, excited for what lay ahead. He later moved to Long Island to raise a family, but after my grandmother died at the age of forty-eight, he returned to the city, finding comfort in its energy. He had hated to leave it.

While Daddy Joe thought the aspirin story was funny, I was uncomfortable with the idea of a world without him. It wasn't only the possibility of my mom never being born, or even myself, but also Captain America—my family's coat of arms. I imagined a giant eraser wiping Captain America from existence, starting with his head, down to his shield, to the toe of his red boot. And then nothing.

✕

Unlike Daddy Joe, I wasn't drawn to the city by ambition or dreams of an exciting future—apartment 1K on West Ninety-Sixth Street, the Upper West Side of Manhattan, was my given home.

First occupied by my paternal great-grandmother Sallie in the 1950s, my dad took over our 550-square-foot apartment in the early seventies. Built in 1937, the building had a pale wood front door that was topped with three art deco arches and three decorative windows. My dad was twentysomething at the time and had secured a job at an eyeglass store, and he was ready to put down some roots with the low rent of $110 a month.

Before Sallie moved into 1K, she was in a studio at the front of the same building. My dad visited her there from the early age of eight and remembers his uneasiness, trying to sleep with the sounds of sirens flying by the window in 1960s New York. He remembers the other buildings now on our block had not yet been built—instead, there were brownstones with crumbling lions on the front banisters. Together, Sallie and my dad took the bus all the way from West Ninety-Sixth Street to Bobo's in Chinatown to enjoy sweet and sour shrimp piled high into a pyramid.

My parents' lives began to intertwine by the time my mom was attending her Long Island high school (my dad ten years older than her). After my dad's family moved to Long Island from Cabrini Boulevard in Washington Heights, his sister entered a Ward Melville High School classroom alongside another new student—my mom's older sister. As the two new kids, they became friendly.

After my grandmother died and my mom and her siblings left for college, their Long Island house became what the local kids called "Hotel California." The house became simply a meeting point for my mom and her orbiting siblings. Daddy Joe moved to his New York City studio apartment in 1975 and rented out rooms to art students from SUNY Stony Brook. My paternal grandfather was an art teacher there, so his kids, my dad included, liked to party with the art students as well. The parties were epic—so epic that my thirty-two-year-old dad made a trip out to attend one with his sister, who had been invited by my mom's older sister.

"He was so drunk," my mom said of my dad. "He was jumping over the couches over and over again. Out of control."

My parents fell in love quickly. My mom moved into apartment 1K only a few months after my parents first met and threw out most of my dad's things—including ex-girlfriends' birth control. Although she was nesting, her intention wasn't to stay in the apartment forever. The day before their City Hall wedding, they fought on a street corner in the West Village about where they would raise a family. My mom wanted a house with a vegetable garden and a few dogs. My dad wanted a rent-controlled apartment in the dense and cultured city. My mom reasoned that she wasn't calling off a wedding the day before on account of this argument, and comforted by Daddy Joe's proximity, she went on with the wedding.

It was in apartment 1K, against the hum of crosstown traffic, that I was raised. Maybe I would have preferred the city as it was when Daddy Joe was a small boy—just beginning to grow, streetcars gliding down Broadway, the islands between the east and west sides of the avenue still clean and barely shaded by young trees, the streetlamps delicate and curved to gently cast light onto the new concrete.

New York in the 1980s was far different from what Daddy Joe had dreamed about as a child. I learned early on that you had to keep an eye on the city.

One afternoon, when I was just six years old, I stood on the corner of Ninety-Sixth and Central Park West, refusing to follow my mom. I wanted to buy a roll of Bonkers candy. She refused. I held my ground, my feet planted underneath me, my hands clutching the hem of my dress. She continued to walk down the sidewalk, threatening to leave me behind if I didn't follow her.

"I'm leaving!" she hollered over her shoulder.

An idea hit—I would leave *her* instead. I spun around and bolted toward the dark staircase of the subway station, my small feet taking me down the first flight of dirty stairs, my curls bouncing with each step. But before the darkness ahead could frighten me, I heard laughter ascending from around the shadowed corner. The faces that appeared were almost as yellow and dusty as the subway tile, and they tilted down toward their hands, focused on the needles they carried. I spun again, this time back up the stairs to my frantic mom.

From that moment on I learned to read the energy of the city and the people around me. It shifted from each block, moving in waves of tension that seemed to hitch a ride on the wind. It's a skill that native New Yorkers develop from an early age—reading strangers' motives in things as small as body language or even the air around them. By the time I was seven, I was able to pick up on the slightest threat.

On another day, while walking west toward Amsterdam Avenue with my dad, the sun orange and fall-like, we passed two men dressed in black sweatpants and black sweatshirts with the hoods pulled over their heads. I locked eyes with one of them. I knew that something was about to happen—that something was brewing inside him, ready to leap out. I could feel his energy, angry and erratic. Years later, I would wonder if our eye contact made them decide to leave us alone and go for the couple behind us. Perhaps that reasoning was another attempt to claim some control over a city that flung itself at me without abandon.

A shriek came from behind us.

"Stop! Get off of him!" a woman screamed.

We turned, and I instinctively clutched my dad's brown leather jacket, my fingers hiding in the warmth of his pocket. He was a sturdy anchor, just as the city began to swell.

One of the men pulled at the woman's purse while the other kicked her husband, who was curled in a ball on the ground, his hands covering his head. People watched; no one moved. The city froze, leaving the four of them to act out this scene for us, their audience.

My dad broke the stillness. "Run back to the apartment and call the police," he ordered.

"What? Why me?"

Before I could protest more, my hand was released from his jacket, and he ran toward them. The two men fled east toward Columbus Avenue, a wallet secured in one of their hands. I ran back to the apartment alone, my heart pounding out of my ears, my stomach sour, my dad already out of view.

TWO

Uptown

1987

✕

New York in the 1980s was unpredictable and angry—a bomb ready to explode at any moment. But sometimes, amid the terrors out on the streets, magic appeared. In through our creaky door came Daddy Joe, his trousers pulled up high and belted near his belly button, his eyes gleaming behind his glasses, and his video camera tucked safely in its black leather carrying case.

The first order of business was to feed him. He was six-three, and although he was as skinny as a beanpole, his love of food was ferocious.

"I got you cold cuts from Zabar's." My mom presented him with a pile of meat and cheese, a fresh baguette, and a container of chopped liver. We watched him eat, as he almost chewed his long fingers with each intense, delighted bite. A muffled moan of approval sent my mom and me into hysterics.

"This is getting pornographic," she said with a laugh, making her way to our narrow, shallow kitchen. The familiar sounds of her dishwashing, the clinks and clanks of silverware against dishes, the soft *clunk* of them being placed in the drying rack, carried throughout the small apartment. I picked at my own sandwich, waiting for Daddy Joe to finish feasting.

Once fed and his fingers wiped clean, Daddy Joe pulled his camera out of its case. "Let's do a tour of the apartment for your sisters," he suggested to my mom.

She agreed, scurrying from wall to wall, putting the final touches on the morning's cleanup. "Let's start in the bedroom."

Before the arrival of my siblings, I had the apartment's only bedroom to myself. Its two windows faced a courtyard in the back of a neighboring building with a concrete wall that kids poked their small heads over to peer in my bedroom window. There was a constant sense of being watched. Throughout the day, you could hear rubber balls bouncing off concrete and children shouting to mothers who hung their heads out of windows. At sunset, a security guard propped open the building's back door and waved everyone in for the night.

"Let's go!" he'd yell. And then silence, except for the wail of sirens and the *scritch-scratch* of pigeons walking across the fire escape landing.

Daddy Joe pulled out a square of black cloth from his bag and wiped the lens of his camera. "Okay, ready?" he asked me. "You're the director."

The video begins with a view of my back. I'm rearranging my Rainbow Brite pony and a Native American doll gifted to me by my mom. She believed that in a past life she had been Native American.

"I got shot in the ass by an arrow," she told me once. "That's how I died."

Fables of death seemed to run in the family. My great-grandmother Rose claimed that her brother Joseph, whom she wanted Daddy Joe named after, had been killed by a horse kicking him in the head while he served as a Cossack in Russia.

"How many Jewish Cossacks were there?!" Daddy Joe laughed in disbelief when retelling the tale.

"Uh, Megan? Can you turn to the camera, please? Want to say anything about those tchotchkes?" Daddy Joe asks.

I continue to touch each toy on my toy chest, making sure they face outward. My cat, Jenny, slithers around my leg.

"Megan, the audience needs to see you," Daddy Joe prods. "Tell us what you're proud of."

I pick up Jenny and turn to face him. Hearing my mom cleaning something behind him, Daddy Joe swings the camera around, but before he can get the lens on her, she is facing the wall like an escaped convict. She hated having her photo taken and learned to move fast when it came to Daddy Joe and the camera that seemed to be surgically attached to his face.

Because of my mom's camera shyness, I take over the tour, albeit silently. Daddy Joe follows me to the dining room, where I have a small desk set up for my artwork. I show him my drawings, wondering if he will see something special in my work—maybe his talent has passed down to me?

On top of the dining room table, tucked between the wall and the napkin holder, sit piles of rolled-up blueprints. My dad, an estimator for construction, liked to work there in the early morning before we woke up. He estimated the cost of renovations for expensive apartments in New York City and rose around 5:30 AM to get work done. Emerging from my bedroom, I'd find him hunched over a spreadsheet and a large blueprint, his thick head of hair not yet graying. When he got up to refill his coffee, I'd study the outlines of the rooms, wishing that the apartment, with all its bedrooms and bathrooms, was being built for us.

Back in the video, Daddy Joe pans to my mom's blue sundress drying on a wire hanger on the kitchen's doorjamb.

"Oh, shit, my dress," she says, taking it down.

He aims the camera at her again, and she scurries out of frame. "That's Jennifer Grey, you know," he tells the video's future audience. In those years, my mom was a dead ringer for her, before Jennifer got her nose job.

Daddy Joe pans back around to the metal railing that separates the dining area from the living room. "Okay, and finally, here is the living room." The camera moves from one wall holding bicycles to the other, where my parents' bed lies. "If you can call it that," he finishes in a mumble.

"I think that's uncalled for!" my mom proclaims from behind him, a hint of laughter with her offense. You can see her leaving the frame as she heads down to the basement with her cart of laundry and bag of quarters.

Then it was just the two of us.

"Now introducing . . . Megan, gymnast! Who is going to perform some gymnasium feats for you," Daddy Joe says.

The video camera is on me, standing in our living room with my hands by my sides, like an Olympian ready to take my turn at the gold.

"Uh, Megan? Do you know what your first feat will be?"

"I'm going to do a flip," I say proudly. I'm beginning to get more comfortable with the camera.

"That sounds really good. I'm going to pan to the mat, and we'll catch you in some action scenes. Okay?"

I nod and walk to the far end of the living room. There's a small couch sitting against the two windows, some artwork, and what looks like a record player sitting on a sheet-covered air conditioner. I take my prep and run the few feet to my parents' bed, a mattress on the floor covered in one of my mom's favorite quilts. I flip quickly, land on my back, and finish with a smile up to the camera and Daddy Joe.

※

Later that afternoon, as my mom walked him out to catch a cab, their shoes slapping against the old marble floors, I watched from the doorway. Without a doorman, carpets, or furniture like the other swank buildings in the neighborhood, our lobby echoed with even the smallest sounds. In the winter, the radiators' loud clanks bounced from wall to ceiling. There was something about the radiators in that building that I loved—their hard work producing that heat was comforting.

My mom and Daddy Joe walked past the silver row of mailboxes, past the creaky elevator with its silver knobs that had to be pressed at least three times to work. The wooden walls of the elevator were scratched by keys, and on the right side of the boxy space, the word "gays" was carved in a slanted angry hand.

"Bye!" I called, my small voice hitting the pale-yellow walls.

I listened to Daddy Joe's booming Kermit the Frog voice recede behind the two heavy front doors of the building. The silence hit hard, the apartment small and dark again.

THREE

Midtown

1989

X

The M11 bus wobbled down Columbus Avenue, taking my mom and me on our journey downtown to Daddy Joe's apartment. It was crowded and hot. I preferred the train for its speediness, but my mom got anxious going underground and through the tunnels. Lucky enough to find two seats together, and already ten minutes into our thirty-minute journey, we settled into vacant stares toward the mid-sections of the standing passengers. Behind the buttons of pants, belt buckles, wrinkled skirts, and bus windows, the city moved slowly—a repetition of street signs and lampposts. My legs weren't quite long enough to touch the ground, leaving my heels to knock against the blue plastic seat.

"Want a piece of gum?" my mom asked, breaking our trance. She was already vigorously chewing some.

"Yeah."

As I turned my head to grab the gum, my eyes caught on a strange sight: tan pants, tan shirt, and, in between, a tan penis. I turned away quickly. Was that a penis? It had to be. My face was red, my heart pulsing all the way down my arms. The man stood nonchalantly, holding the metal railing with one hand, while his other hand hung lifeless, like his exposed penis. It was just another day for him. Just him and his penis out for a bus ride.

Only eight years old and embarrassed by the presence of a penis, I didn't say a word. I spent the remainder of the ride with my eyes fixed on my lap, praying that my mom wouldn't notice.

At Fifty-Seventh Street and Ninth Avenue, we got off the bus and walked the one block to Daddy Joe's building. It was a face of windows, with thin lines of brick between each floor—like the cross-hatching from his comic book art.

With the never-ending energy of a child, and in an attempt to shake off the penis sighting, I ran up the brick steps at full speed, climbing over the circular concrete benches that dotted the front courtyard of his building. Hooking my hand around the lamppost with its four large round bulbs, I spun my body and then ran back to the bench to begin my obstacle course again.

"Let's go," my mom called impatiently from the door.

The doorman, Ralph, was holding it open with his back, smiling beneath a black cap. I did one last swing, enjoying the effort of fighting gravity.

"Hello, Ms. Megan!" Ralph patted the top of my head. "Can you give some mail to your grandpa?"

It was just past 11:00 AM when my mom let us into Daddy Joe's apartment with her key. He was still asleep. Aside from the faint snores from his bedroom, the apartment was quiet. The almost-noon light illuminated dust motes swirling above canisters of paintbrushes, pens, and scraps of paper on the drawing table.

"Wake him up," she said. "It's late."

I pushed open the bedroom door just enough to catch a glimpse of him sleeping. He was tangled in a worn blanket filled with down, his feet sticking out the bottom, cradling each other as if to keep from falling off the edge of the bed. Years later, as an adult waking in my

Boston bed, I noticed how my feet spooned each other in the same way, my pale calves almost identical to Daddy Joe's.

"Daddy Joe, we're here," I whispered from the doorway.

After a few sharp, quick snores, he slowly climbed out of his dream. "Hi, baby. What time is it? I need coffee."

He pulled himself out of bed with a few faux screams of effort and headed to the bathroom for a loud morning pee accented by a fart. I heard the sink turn on as he splashed some water on his face, looked in the mirror, and screamed like a woman: "I'm so ugly!" A dramatic stumble to the kitchen, and he was up. The sound of his ancient coffeemaker gurgling to life signaled the official start of his day.

I was only three days old when I first visited Daddy Joe's apartment. Roosevelt Hospital, where I was born, was a few blocks away. One of the first photographs of me was taken in his kitchen, my dad holding my small body in his palms like a loaf of bread. I was the first grandchild in the family, and so my nickname for Daddy Joe, coined when I was about five years old, stuck.

His kitchen table—really a small desk against the wall—was covered in containers of almonds, sugar-free candy, and old copies of the *New York Post*. Taking up most of his living room was the drawing table—covered with notes, doodles, old pens and pencils—that solidified how special he was to the rest of the world. That was where he became Joe Simon, the comic book legend.

On his wall, above his electric typewriter, there were a number of pieces of art, one of them a portrait of him done by Stan Kaye, a comic book artist most known for his work on the Superman comics beginning in 1945.

"This was when I was young and handsome," Daddy Joe said. "Stan has since deceased—probably while drawing this ugly face." He laughed and then stopped abruptly. "That's not funny. Rest in peace, Stan."

While my mom did the pile of dishes in the sink, I stood beside him at his drawing table. His morning breath, mixed with coffee, seemed to form a cloud above us as he unearthed a sheet of paper from the night before. It was the start of a Captain America sketch that showed the hero leaping across the page. I could watch Daddy Joe move over the paper forever, shifting my weight from one leg to the other, listening to my mom trying to make sense of his kitchen and the mess of his late-night cooking escapades.

Daddy Joe was especially proud of his use of perspective. "You see how this leg looks shorter?" His pen rested between his index and third fingers, his elbow on the table.

I nodded. I had surely been given this lesson many times before. But I didn't say that. I let him be the teacher and kept my eyes on his movements over the page.

"It's so that it looks farther away." His long fingers held the pencil over the sketch so naturally that it seemed the pencil and his hand were simply an extension of each other. "Now we have to add color."

"Father, this apartment is filthy," my mom whined from the kitchen.

Daddy Joe looked at me, a glint in his eyes. Swiveling around in his chair, he reached behind a pile of paper and pulled out two large porcini mushrooms.

"Lori!" he yelled. "Lori, what's growing in here?"

"What the fuck is this?" she called from the stove, peering into his beloved pressure cooker, ignoring the one-man act.

"Lori? Just leave it," he pleaded, putting down the mushrooms.

"What *is* it?"

"Cow tongue."

My mom looked at me, Daddy Joe now focused on his sketch again, and mimed a gag. "I'm throwing it out," she declared.

"Lori? If you touch it, I'll put *you* in the pot."

He got up from the table to save his cow tongue, taking the two mushrooms with him. I took his seat, pulling out a fresh piece of paper to practice his autograph—the oblong "o" and the sharp three lines for the "e" in Joe.

)(

When Daddy Joe first arrived in New York City, he worked freelance assignments retouching publicity photos for Paramount Pictures in Times Square. But he was soon tired of the tedious work and continued his search for a more creative position. He found something better with Macfadden Publications, one of the largest magazine publishers in the country.

Daddy Joe quickly proved his talent to his boss, Harlan Crandall, by doing spot illustrations—drawings of small items like household objects and guns to decorate the pages. These were easy enough to do, and he was quickly promoted to crime illustrations for magazines like *True Detective*. After Daddy Joe worked for Macfadden for only a year, Crandall suggested that he speak to his friend Lloyd Jacquet, the head of Funnies, Inc. A comic book packager of the 1930s and '40s, Funnies, Inc. created the characters, script, art, and lettering for comic books, and then sold them to publishers.

Jacquet gave Daddy Joe his very first comic book assignment—a seven-page Western—and soon after, Daddy Joe created his first comic book, *The Fiery Mask*, about a man named Jack Castle, who gains superhuman strength and whose eyes are transformed into twin flamethrowers via a mysterious green light. Daddy Joe loved the world of fantasy, realizing each day that this was the perfect profession for him. He had found his calling.

In 1939, after Daddy Joe moved from Funnies to Fox Publications, his good friend Alfred Harvey (who would one day start Harvey Comics) introduced him to Jacob Kurtzberg—later known as Jack Kirby. At the time, the three of them were working in the bullpen at Fox Publications, but Daddy Joe hadn't yet spoken to Jack—he had only admired from afar Jack's work on Blue Beetle. Because it was the Depression, Daddy Joe took on freelance gigs outside of his day job. One day, Al told Daddy Joe that Jack wanted to get in on these gigs.

"Send him over," Daddy Joe told Al, a cigar between his teeth.

When Jack approached Daddy Joe's drawing table, he apologized for being pudgy, saying he was a victim of the Danish—Danish pastries. Daddy Joe knew immediately that they would become great friends.

Daddy Joe and Jack began working late nights together on freelance assignments. If they didn't have an assignment, they built up their inventory with new material—new characters or storylines—and shelved it to be sold at a later date. They sometimes worked all night, doing everything themselves: inking, erasing, even lettering. They loved the comic book business, their passion powering them from one project to the next.

Daddy Joe was twenty-four, and Jack was twenty-two. During that time, Batman was a huge success, mostly due to the villains in the storyline. They began to think that maybe this was the way to create the next big hit—rather than brainstorming about who the hero should be, Daddy Joe began with the villain. Newspapers were filled with stories from Europe, and so Daddy Joe thought to himself, *Why not use a real-life villain?*

"Adolf Hitler would be the perfect foil for our next new character, what with his hair and that stupid-looking moustache and his goose-stepping," he wrote in his memoir.

Who would be Hitler's foil? It would have to be someone patriotic, an all-American hero decked out in red, white, and blue gear. The character they created, one of those unused characters sitting on the shelf, waiting to be sold, was Steve Rogers, Captain America, a courageous young man whose powers came from a shot. Rogers was likely inspired by Daddy Joe's character Blue Bolt, who is healed by a radium treatment after being struck by lightning, attaining the ability to project lightning bolts.

Daddy Joe's imagination was always on. He thought up the villainous Red Skull while sitting in New York's Childs Restaurant, eating a hot-fudge sundae. As he watched the fudge melt, he became intrigued and started some sketches on the place mat, transforming the drips into arms and legs. *I'll call him Hot Fudge*, he thought.

"You have to be stupid to be in this business," he later joked.

He gave up on the fudge but moved on to the cherry on top, and the shape and bright color sparked the idea for the Red Skull. He didn't think this villain would last more than one issue, but, he said, "You never know what people are going to be attracted to!"

After Daddy Joe got a call from Martin Goodman of Timely Comics with a job offer in late 1939, he left Fox Publications and made sure to get Jack Kirby a job at Timely as well. One of the first things Daddy Joe did was show Goodman the sketch of Captain America. With the character's patriotic garb and mission to defeat the Nazis, Goodman knew it was a sure thing. But he also knew that the first issue needed to be printed and distributed quickly. God forbid they release it too late—after their villain, Hitler, was already dead. The production of the first issue was put on the fast track, Daddy Joe the ringleader, finding the help that he and Jack needed to make it happen.

The first issue of *Captain America Comics*, with the hero punching Hitler in the jaw, was created almost one year before the United States entered World War II. Because Hitler was alive, putting him on the cover of a comic book (and being punched, to boot) was a daring move. Hitler's supporters weren't only in Europe; there were many Nazi sympathizers in America. After getting threatening phone calls to their Timely office, and strange men lurking out in front of their office building, everyone at Timely started to get nervous.

In his book *The Comic Book Makers*, Daddy Joe tells the story about getting a phone call from the then mayor of New York, Fiorello La Guardia. La Guardia promised to protect them and sent police officers to stand guard at their office building.

"You can't take shit from anyone," Daddy Joe used to say.

I usually laughed when he said this, his lanky frame making him anything but threatening. But I came to realize just how daring the comic book cover was, and the bravery it took Daddy Joe and Jack to put their opinions front and center.

X

Done with the dishes, the mess of his kitchen desk quickly organized, my mom took a scrap of paper from Daddy Joe's drawing table. "What do you want from the store?" she asked him, pen in hand.

"Just get me the usual," he said, now in his leather chair, coffee still in hand.

"Megan, do you want to come with me or stay here?"

"Stay here," I said. I was done practicing his autograph and was now working on a picture of a red barn. Of course I wanted to stay.

"Megan and I will talk business," Daddy Joe said.

After the door of his apartment closed behind my mom, we let the silence sit between us for a moment.

"Is that a barn?" Daddy Joe asked.

"Yeah."

"Uh-huh, very nice."

The morning sun rested on his coffee-less hand, the side of it smudged with ink. The clock clicked above his TV. He reached for the remote to turn on the TV.

I got up and wandered to his bedroom, where he kept a drawer of VHS tapes labeled with yellowed masking tape. I touched each one with my finger—*A Chorus Line*, *The Wizard of Oz*—before finally deciding on *Bye Bye Birdie*. After inserting the tape and bringing his bedroom TV to life, I lay in the middle of his bed, the pillow still warm from his head. I stayed on his bed, and he stayed in his chair for an hour—the edges of our bubbles touching, a gentle reminder that we were still there with each other.

When my mom returned from the grocery store, I begged her to let me stay longer. She agreed, saying she would pick me up in a few hours.

Daddy Joe and I headed over to a food festival a few blocks away, the smell of sausage and onions as thick as the crowd. He bought me fried dough, the powdered sugar clinging to my fingertips, my tongue warm and slick from the grease. We climbed up on a comically large armchair for a photo, holding oversize props, me with a tennis racket and him with a can of beer. He later taped it to the door of his freezer, where I often went looking for ice-cream bars and where he kept a wad of cash wrapped in tinfoil shoved in the back corner.

"Do you have any quarters?" my mom asked Daddy Joe when she returned to pick me up.

"Just got some new rolls," he said. "In my underwear drawer."

She stuffed two rolls in the front of her backpack, enough for a few weeks of laundry. "Let's go, Megan. I have to get back to make dinner."

"Daddy Joe got me fried dough," I said proudly.

My mom scrunched her face. "So greasy."

"Bye, baby," Daddy Joe said, and settled back at his drawing table, searching under the scraps of paper for something.

"Bye, Father," my mom called as the two of us walked out his door and back down the popcorn-walled hallway, leaving him to his work.

FOUR

Beyond Apartment 1K

1989–1990

Ж

I was making baby powder pancakes on the radiator in the bedroom when the phone rang. After pouring the baby-powder-and-water mixture into small mounds on the radiator cover, I waited patiently for them to cook. Later my mom would scrub the radiators, her annoyance with my mess giving her the needed elbow grease.

The phone continued to ring. I was deep in a fantasy, cooking in a remote forest cabin, like Laura Ingalls from *Little House on the Prairie*. This was a recurring theme in my play. During school recess in Central Park, I climbed the gray rocks on the edge of the East Meadow, looking for rainwater pooled in the many nooks and crannies. Once found, the water became my kitchen sink, and I spent most of the hour stirring the muck with twigs. Other times, at the playground with the yellow slide, I eyed the crack vials littered around the edges of the sand and under the green wooden benches. My imagination turned them into tiny cups for my cottage kitchen, but my fantasy quickly imploded and the vials were dropped with a shout from my horrified mom.

My pancake fantasy began to deteriorate with the ringing phone, and I realized that my mom was still in the basement doing laundry. I left my pancakes and headed for the phone at the front of the apartment.

"Hello?" I looked up at the chalkboard on the wall with the scribbled to-do list. *Call doc, milk, pay electric.*

"Lori?" I heard a strained voice whisper my mom's name.

"No. Who is this?" I asked, pressing the receiver against my ear, my small fingers clutching the black coiled phone cord. The voice sounded familiar.

"Megan? Help me."

It was our thirtysomething-year-old neighbor David. My mom liked to lean against our doorjamb and gossip with him about the other neighbors. Sometimes she left a bag of leftover baked goods hanging from his bronze doorknob, waiting for him to return home. I wondered why he was calling when his apartment was right next to ours, so close we shared a wall. I then remembered the night before, when I heard my mom telling my dad that David was in the hospital, losing his battle to AIDS, probably doped up on morphine.

"Hello?" was all I could say, pretending not to hear him. I pictured him sweaty and delirious in his hospital bed, tangled in the stiff white sheets, his almost-white hair plastered to his forehead. I didn't want to be on the phone anymore.

"Help me. I'm bleeding." He sounded as if he were in the depths of a bad dream, not speaking directly to me, but up to the heavens.

His words left me breathless. I swiftly hung up.

David died the next day. Even though he wasn't coherent when he called, I felt guilty for hanging up. He must not have had any family to call, and so he thought of my mom in his morphine dream. I'd deserted him in his last hours. I wondered if he would haunt me. I deserved it.

That weekend, my mom and I watched as two strangers cleaned out David's apartment, the dark hardwood floor bare and erased of the man who had lived there. Even after we stopped watching and went back into our apartment, we could hear the sounds of drawers opening and shutting and furniture grinding against the floor through our shared wall.

※

At eight years old, I was having nightmares of finding myself on a different floor of the building. In the dreams, the hallway looked eerily familiar, but I knew in my gut that it wasn't my floor. It was like a different world, one in which I wasn't welcome. Who lived behind all those doors? How would I figure out how to get back to my own apartment?

I was the lone child in the building. My family only spoke to a few neighbors back then, while the others completely ignored us. One man, John, also known as the Man with the Wild Dogs, would always exit the elevator, tripping over his gang of canines. He never said a word to us as he walked past, his feet hidden by the grunting, drooling dogs eager to take a piss.

When I came down with strep throat, my mom took me to the doctor, and by the time we got home from the appointment, my fever had begun to soar. I was so exhausted that I fainted in the middle of our lobby. My mom, small-framed, stood there trying to figure out how to lift me and get me into the apartment. I was only unconscious for a moment, but even after I regained consciousness, I was too feverish to get up and walk on my own. As my mom yanked my arm, begging me to get up, her pleading voice echoing off the marble floors and mirrored wall, the Man with the Wild Dogs stepped out of the elevator.

Relieved to see another adult, she dropped my arm and looked at him helplessly. Holding the bouquet of leashes in his outstretched hand, he aimed the dogs to walk around us and all but stepped over my body.

Although David was friendly, greeting me with a smile every time he saw me in the hallway—sometimes even giddily lifting me up in the air by my armpits—with his shrinking frame and graying skin, I was scared of him. He worked down on Forty-Second Street, before it was a tourist destination. He was a well-known adult entertainer, his picture on posters around the Times Square neighborhood. Back in our building, he sometimes lost himself in what seemed to be a psychological disorder, urinating or sprinkling lighter fluid on the apartment doors. Beneath my mom's friendliness, I could sense her uneasiness around him, like he was a sick animal, unpredictable. This only fueled my fear of him, of what he represented—things like death, which I saw only in scary movies. His phone call proved that my fears about what lay beyond could penetrate our apartment door.

X

One year after the phone call from David, during a typical morning at the bus stop, I stood with some friends from my fourth-grade class. Eric silently watched the ground, his hands on the straps of his backpack, while Sean and I talked about the school baseball game from the day before.

"Did you see how the pitcher just threw the ball directly at my head?" I asked. "It's because I'm the only girl on the team."

"Yeah, that's messed up," Sean said, leaning toward the road, crosstown traffic racing by, looking for the yellow school bus that would wind us through Central Park to the East Side. The driver liked to flip his eyelids inside out, the pink flesh causing us to squeal in horror.

"Pretty dumb, because it just got me on base."

We laughed; I saw Eric smile.

And then Eric was in the air, lifted off the ground in a bear hug by a strange man. Sean and I froze, watching Eric move toward the sky and the windows of the building that we stood in front of. Before we could scream for help, or even register what was happening, the man set Eric down and sprinted off. That's where the scene ends in my memory, like a movie fading to black.

A few weeks later, a neighbor informed my parents that *60 Minutes* wanted to interview us about the man wreaking havoc on our Upper West Side neighborhood. Head filled with dreams of on-screen stardom, I nodded and agreed to tell my friend's horrific bear-hug story.

They called him the "Wild Man of 96th Street" or "Crazy Larry." He set fires under cars, heaved rocks through stained-glass church windows, masturbated in front of kids, and threatened elderly people with a nail-studded club. He once took the marble bench from the lobby of the building where my best friend lived and heaved it into the windshield of a parked car and then defecated in its back seat. Larry was a crack addict who was in and out of treatment, and residents were fed up with the system and its inability to keep him from coming back to the neighborhood for monthly jaunts.

Daddy Joe eagerly waited for our *60 Minutes* episode to air so that he could record it on a VHS tape. He collected blank tapes for recording HBO movies, so we were frequently visiting Radio Shack to restock his supply.

That Sunday, I sat at his drawing table while he unsheathed a brand-new tape. As the football game that was airing was ending, he gently wiped the tape, tested the two gears with black film wrapped around them, and then inserted it into his video player. At 6:59 PM, he ceremoniously hit record. We watched the episode together, the sound turned up, the video player humming as it recorded.

"He just grabbed him. Just grabbed him," I told Lesley Stahl from a folding chair in a neighbor's apartment. I wore a blue cotton dress to match my eyes.

"Were you scared?" Lesley asked gently. I nodded and offered only a whimper of a yes.

When the show cut to commercial, Daddy Joe yelped with excitement from his leather chair. "You're a star!" he exclaimed. "So beautiful." His balding head pressed against the headrest. "Now let's see if this fucking thing worked."

He rocked himself forward, dramatically groaning as he got himself out of the chair to check the recording. I grinned proudly from the black swivel chair behind his drawing table, taking a bite of my Chinese spareribs.

X

With Daddy Joe's enthusiasm and love for the city, I was constantly trying to find the balance between loving and embracing it the way he did and dodging what felt like relentless terrors. It helped that Daddy Joe spoiled me with all that New York had to offer.

"Where do you want to go today?" he'd asked me.

That was easy—FAO Schwarz.

After bolting both locks of his apartment door, he danced toward the elevators, throwing his hands in the air singing, "Here comes the judge, here comes the judge!"—his imitation of Sammy Davis Jr. on *Laugh-In*.

We walked the streets together, heading east, me running to keep up with his long strides. Often he'd strike up a conversation with a stranger, leaving me to stand impatiently by his side. I was itching to get to the toy store, to ride the escalator under the big clock singing "Welcome to Our World of Toys."

Even running errands with him was an adventure. At least once a month he walked over to Lee's Art Shop to get some supplies for his re-creations. They loved him there. He was greeted with smiles and handshakes before he ogled the newest pens and paintbrushes. He had a glow to him in there, like me in FAO Schwarz.

As a young adult, Daddy Joe ran to the city the first chance he got, so I knew that beyond the terrors of the city lay something special. He made everything exciting—worth experiencing. But growing up in New York and being shaped by the city during my formative years— coming of age having seen a stranger's penis on the bus, just casually hanging out of his tan, penis-colored slacks like a perverted GI Joe— was something totally different. The city wasn't quite the same entity to Daddy Joe as it was to me. I had to figure out how to find a balance between the versions of New York we each knew.

5

Uptown to Upstate

1990

※

The phone was hidden under my mom's curls, held between her shoulder and her ear. I could hear Daddy Joe's voice, hitting high notes of doubt. It was never easy for him to leave the city.

"Father, just come with us," she said. "It's only for a week."

More indecision on his end of the phone. My mom clucked her tongue in exasperation.

"Father," she said firmly, "you can freeze the brisket and make it when you get home."

It was settled. He was coming with us to a rented cabin close to my aunt Gail's house in Skaneateles, about five hours north in upstate New York. It was a trip we did at least once a year, usually staying in Gail's house. It smelled like her two large Newfoundland dogs, both of which sniffed our crotches and drooled on our knees. Her backyard, up a steep hill from the lake—one of eleven Finger Lakes in the region—was covered in fossils. All you had to do was look down to find at least four different slabs of rock, indented with the form of some long-ago creature. That year, though, my parents had decided to rent a cabin.

Daddy Joe insisted on renting a car. He didn't trust the cars my parents owned to make the journey, and they never argued with him.

My dad left our apartment the morning of our departure to pick him up, get the rental car, and then drive back uptown to gather the rest of us and the luggage.

Outside our building, Daddy Joe waited in the front seat of the tan rental car, his forearm resting on the open window.

"Hi, Father," my mom said, swinging her leather backpack onto the back seat. I followed behind her, grinning at the sight of Daddy Joe.

"Like the car?" he asked.

"Very nice," she answered absentmindedly as she sorted through her bag for a Mento Mint to soothe her stomach. I held out my hand for one. We shared the same stomach.

"I want you to know, Lori, that I'm going to drive it at some point during this trip."

"Dream on, old man," she shot back. I giggled. I loved their banter.

My car sickness began only twenty minutes into our drive thanks to the stop and go of city traffic. I prayed that Daddy Joe would stop talking; each word out of his mouth sent my stomach lurching for my throat.

"Lori, that yogurt drink you got me is so good!" he bellowed to the back of the car.

"So good, right?" my mom shouted back to the front.

"Any other flavors? Chocolate?"

Dear god, make it stop.

Soon, he quieted, only the soft sounds of *Car Talk*—a discussion on replacing alternators—mumbling out of the radio speakers. I passed out with a piece of gum resting against my teeth, my stomach easing back to normal.

That week, Daddy Joe and I made it a nightly ritual to sit down by the lake with the stars bright over our heads. I squatted over the rocky shoreline, breaking twigs in half, stacking everything in just the right way to make a small campfire. I ignored his concerns over my obsession with fire and lit the mound of sticks with his lighter. I loved the snap of the lighter as the flint worked to spark and the clank of the lighter's lid once the job was accomplished. Despite his concerns, Daddy Joe let me light his cigar, checking to see if it was evenly lit after a few test pulls.

Once the fire was well on its way and his cigar successfully lit, he told me stories from my mom's childhood; about the large houses they lived in, about the many Great Danes they raised, and, of course, about Harriet, the grandmother I never met. She was a mystery to me, a missing puzzle piece to who my mom was and also who Daddy Joe was—this woman he'd loved and chosen as a wife.

As he recounted many times before, after returning from the war in 1945 (he had served with the Coast Guard on mounted beach patrol, scanning the Jersey shoreline for enemy ships from horseback), he was called into Alfred Harvey's office. Harvey, it turned out, wanted the Simon and Kirby team to join his company, Harvey Comics, the home of successful characters such as Wendy the Good Little Witch and Casper the Friendly Ghost. As Daddy Joe sat in the waiting room, a secretary with auburn hair seated at a desk across from him leaned over to look at his trousers.

"Pull up your pant leg," she ordered.

"What?"

"Just pull up your pant leg," she said with a smile. "Past the knee."

He pulled it up.

"That's good," she said, sitting back in her chair.

Daddy Joe went into his meeting, but as he left, he asked her what that was about.

"I wouldn't go out with a guy who had white, pasty legs."

And that's how Daddy Joe met my grandmother Harriet.

"Do I look like her?" I asked him.

"Not really," he said, and my heart dropped. I was desperate for some sort of connection to her. If I reminded Daddy Joe of Harriet, then maybe he would love me as much as he loved her. Maybe it would make our bond even stronger—more special.

"You do have the same exact hair color as her, though," he added. It was only hair color, but it was something.

"I remember sitting in the library, and the librarian came up to me to let me know I had a phone call." Daddy Joe took a pull from his cigar. "The librarian asked me for my autograph. I said, 'How did you know who I am?' Turns out Harriet had called looking for 'Joe Simon, creator of Captain America.'" He laughed up to the starry sky.

"How long did you date Harriet until you knew you wanted to marry her?" I asked.

"There was no dating with Harriet. If she liked you, that was it. You were hers."

Maybe that was something else we had in common, my mysterious grandmother and me. I had met Daddy Joe when I was only three days old, but I guess I'd known even then that he was someone to hold on to with everything that I had.

I pictured Harriet up there, looking down on us. I wondered if she were still alive, if she would be sitting with us. I wondered if Daddy Joe would be a different person altogether, without the heart-break and loss. I thought of him still living on Long Island, in their Stony Brook house, and not being a quick subway ride away from my own apartment. I appreciated, even at that young age, the color—the brightness—he brought to my life. Daddy Joe's magic wasn't just on the pages of his colorful comics. It followed him wherever he went.

He stubbed out the cigar on a rock. "It's getting late. Throw some water on that fire."

I cupped my hands and dipped them into the ice-cold lake water. The fire hissed its way out, sending thick smoke up to the sky.

The next day, we all went for a walk and stopped at an old cemetery. I was fascinated by the gray headstones, many of them cracked, some toppled over with age. Large sugar maples towered over us, offering some shade and relief from the summer sun.

"Look, this one was just a kid," I pointed out. The headstone was small. I learned that the smaller headstones usually marked a child's grave.

"It's nice here," my mom said, looking up at the trees.

"So nice," Daddy Joe agreed.

"You can put me here," she offered.

"Definitely." Daddy Joe lifted the video camera to his right eye. "It's right next to the supermarket."

Ж

While he hated to leave the city, the excitement of a comic convention and meeting fans, being in his element, was enough to get Daddy Joe back in the front seat of a car.

That winter, we headed back upstate to a comic convention in Ithaca. When we arrived at the hotel, a generic Marriott or Hilton with cheap blue carpet and a faux wooden front desk, my mom called, "See you later, honeymooners!" over her shoulder as Daddy Joe and I headed to our shared room. I watched him unlock our room door, giddy with excitement for our next few hours together. Our hotel stays usually consisted of watching too much TV and walking to the closest supermarket to buy cooked shrimp with cocktail sauce, which we stored, to my mom's disgust, in a bucket of ice on the hotel room desk.

The next day, at the convention, I parked myself next to Daddy Joe at a white plastic table as he signed autographs. I folded a piece of paper and made a sign to place next to his: Megan, granddaughter of Joe Simon.

"You must be very proud of your grandpa," a fan said to me, smiling. "I'd love to get your autograph, too."

Thrilled, I scribbled my name on his scrap of paper.

"Megan taught me everything I know," Daddy Joe told the fan. They shared a laugh, and I sat taller, adjusting my ponytail before the next person approached our table.

Afterward, we left Ithaca and headed north to Aunt Gail's house in Skaneateles, where Daddy Joe filmed my dad and me in her backyard. The fossils were now buried under snow. As my dad patted and sculpted a snowman's round belly, I got an idea. Hiding behind the snowman, I formed a few snowballs with my already soaked gloves. While Daddy Joe was distracted with the zoom feature on the camera, I made my attack, missing him with the first three and then *whack*, his coat took a hit. My giddy shrieks were high in the air before Daddy Joe slipped and fell, laughing the whole way down, landing on his ass.

I panicked that I'd gone too far. Had I done the unthinkable and broken him? For a few seconds, as he got his bearings, he looked pissed. He got himself up, grabbed the camera off the snow-covered ground, and brought it up to his eye.

"Still works!" he declared with delight. I breathed again.

In the car ride back to the city, we told the story to my mom, Daddy Joe embellishing the story for dramatic effect—his true talent.

"She pushed me!"

"I did not!" I screamed, still slightly mortified that I'd made him fall and grateful for his good humor.

Soon, everyone was lulled by the monotony of the scenery. It wasn't until the buildings started getting taller and the city came into view that Daddy Joe was energized. Excited by our approach, he began to sing Sinatra's "New York, New York."

Daddy Joe's mother had wanted a singer in the family, so when he was a child, she had once crossed her fingers and asked him to sing something. He belted out only a few notes before she said, "Never mind, you're tone-deaf." Despite his mother's disapproval so many years earlier, he believed he was a beautiful singer.

"'It's up to you! New York!'" he hollered as we coasted down the West Side Highway.

Now in front of his building, Daddy Joe lumbered toward his lair.

"I'll call you tomorrow!" my mom shouted to him as she moved from the back seat to the front of the car. I watched him predictably turn a sharp left to check his mailbox, a long metal slot that ate three quarters of his arm. He liked to open the royalty checks right there in front of the doorman and shout out the ridiculous amount with excitement. "Wow! Fifty-four cents! I'm rich!" He had one for two cents taped to his apartment door.

With Daddy Joe back in his apartment, like an electronic device back in its charging port, my dad pulled us into the moving traffic and we headed uptown toward home. I slunk down in the back seat, another adventure, another escape, with Daddy Joe behind me.

SIX

He's Only Human, After All

1991

X

The Neubert Ballet Company held classes for aspiring ballerinas in the sepia-toned Carnegie Hall building on Fifty-Sixth Street and Seventh Avenue. At ten years old, I was one of those dancers, heading to class a few times a week after school let out.

My mom dropped me off in the humid dressing room, where I pulled on my leotard and tights. After saying her goodbyes, she usually walked a few avenues over to hang out with Daddy Joe. But now, eight months pregnant with my brother, she was tired and considered simply finding a bench to rest on instead.

"Something told me to go," she told me years later.

I chatted with the other girls while pushing a few dozen bobby pins into my messy bun, finishing it off with a light brown hairnet. We filed into the dance studio, still warm from the previous class. The smooth gray floor, spacious and bare, felt full of possibilities—a respite from my small apartment and the crowded city.

I moved in the dance studio joyously. I loved the way my pink slippers slid against the floor, the sound almost velvety. I could stretch the energy from my legs all the way through the ends of my toes, from my shoulders out through the tips of my fingers. I was good at dancing. Ms. Neubert often asked me to show the class a routine across the floor.

"Beautiful!" she shouted toward me as I moved. "Watch her musicality," she told the class. I tried not to beam too brightly by her compliments.

At the end of class, I didn't find my mom waiting outside the dressing room as she usually did. Instead, I saw Ann, a friend of hers.

"Where's my mom?" I asked, sweat still dampening my forehead.

"Honey, your grandfather wasn't feeling well, so your mom took him to the hospital. I'm going to take you there now, okay?"

I nodded wordlessly and followed her down the hallway to the elevators, my backpack creating a pool of sweat between my shoulder blades.

⋊⋉

The moment my mom stepped out of the elevator onto his floor, she heard his TV screaming at the end of the hall. It made her heart jump into her throat—she knew something wasn't right. With her hand holding the underside of her large belly, she hurried to his door and pushed it open. The apartment was shrouded in darkness. Beneath the sounds of the TV, she heard pots and pans banging together in the kitchen.

"Father?" she called into the void.

He was muttering to himself. She flipped the light switch and saw him standing in his boxers, delirious, incoherent, trying to make soup in his pressure cooker. His stomach was distended, almost as big as hers.

"Father?" she tried again.

He continued muttering. After turning off the TV, she touched his aging forearm, covered in liver spots, trying to wake him from what seemed to be a dream. His skin was burning hot.

When the ambulance came, they asked Daddy Joe who the president was. "Hillary," he said.

"He probably had a stroke," the paramedics told my mom as they wheeled him out his apartment door. She followed them, still clutching her belly, nervous about what the stress would do to her pregnancy.

Daddy Joe was sent for X-rays of his distended stomach. It wasn't a stroke. His temperature was 106—he had an infection from a chicken bone piercing his intestines.

"He wouldn't have made it through the night. He's lucky you found him," the doctor told my mom.

I followed Ann through the halls of Roosevelt Hospital, passing a long row of curtains and gurneys, some with people lying on them. I kept my eyes to the ground. The sight of all the sick people and the overwhelming sense of pain and suffering made my stomach turn.

Soon I could hear my mom's voice, and then Daddy Joe's.

"Did you hear what the doctor said about your prescription?" she asked him from behind a blue curtain.

"Huh? Oh, yes. Yes," he answered tiredly.

Ann pulled back the curtain, and Daddy Joe looked up at me from the bed, another curtain separating him from his coughing roommate. My mom sat beside him in a plastic chair, her leather backpack on her lap between her interwoven fingers and her stomach. We were both in hell.

"Hi, baby. Like my new dress?" Daddy Joe asked, referring to his blue hospital gown.

I smiled, but it was only to please him. I didn't want to be there. I didn't want to see him so vulnerable. I had the growing urge to turn and run from him. Here, in the hospital where I was born, I understood just how human he was—how delicate a life could be, no matter how loved the person was.

Earlier that year, on April Fool's Day, I had told my teacher that my grandfather died. We were standing in the middle of Central Park's East Meadow, and he put his hand on my shoulder.

"I'm so sorry," he almost whispered.

"I'm just kidding. April Fool's!"

His face dropped. "That's not funny."

I was mortified. But I was also incredibly ignorant of the fact that Daddy Joe could leave us at any time. It seemed so impossible that I said those words without fear. Seeing Daddy Joe in the hospital was a surefire way to slap some sense into me. Just one more night alone and he would have been gone.

)(

At the time, my experience with death was limited. I had never met my grandmother Harriet; she was simply a void of a grandmother that I was born with. My paternal grandfather had died when I was only four years old, though I remembered visiting him in the upstairs bedroom of my grandparents' house, where he was hooked up to an oxygen tank to help him breathe through his lung cancer. SUNY Stony Brook had put together an art exhibit after his death, and my dad had held me as he walked from one piece of art to the next. My legs were wrapped around his waist, my head resting on his shoulder while I sleepily clutched my lovey, a small piece of rainbow cloth, and sucked my thumb.

My paternal great-grandmother Sallie had died around that time as well. I knew her only from a few visits down to Miami, where I slept with my parents in the living room of her condo, terrified of the most intense thunderstorm I had ever experienced. It was also from the balcony of her condo that I saw my first double rainbow. When she died, it was one of the few times I'd ever seen my dad cry. He sat on the edge of my twin-size bed to tell me she was gone, next to my stuffed bear that I'd named Bucky. I was more upset by the tears rolling down his face.

The sorrow that my dad showed for the loss of his grandmother seemed a bit strange to me. I held the belief that unless it was a parent or sibling, the death of a relative, especially an older one, shouldn't be that intense. But as I got older, the years with Daddy Joe piling on top of one another, our bond growing stronger, I worried that I was wrong. With the new reality that he would one day die and leave us, my love for him began to terrify me.

X

A few weeks after the chicken bone incident, Daddy Joe and I sat across from each other in Ralph's Ristorante Italiano. It was one of our favorite spots, only a short walk from his apartment. While we waited for our food, I doodled on the white paper place mat with crayons the waiter had given me. Daddy Joe watched me, his long fingers tapping the table.

"Let me have a few of those," he said, taking the blue crayon. He began to sketch the head of Captain America. Although it wasn't one of his fancy pencils, his hand still moved swiftly, loosely—confidently. This, to me, was the epitome of a true artist. I wished that I could move over the paper like that, but instead the lines of the house I'd drawn were rigid and overly thought out. I decided to try again, flipping over the place mat, and began to sketch Daddy Joe's face, starting with his large-framed glasses, moving my hand as quickly as possible.

He laughed when he realized what I was doing. "Megan, don't you know I'm too ugly to draw?"

The waiter arrived with our sodas, predictably smiling down at Daddy Joe's sketch. It was now filling out, the bold lines and color making it appear to pop off the paper.

"Wow, that's great," the waiter said.

"Are you a Captain America fan?" Daddy Joe asked him, his crayon paused at Cap's shoulder.

"Of course!"

"Well, then," Daddy Joe said, signing his name in the bottom corner, "this is yours—from the creator of Captain America."

I put down my crayon and continued to study Daddy Joe as I sipped my Pepsi. I thought of him on that hospital bed. What a relief it was to have him back, to be sitting across from him at our favorite restaurant again. But the fear of losing him was more than a newly planted seed. It had roots now, threatening to take hold.

From that point on, there was hesitation to my visits, a reluctance to allow myself the comfort of his apartment and the familiarity of his dry humor. I foolishly wondered if there was a way to keep him from meaning too much, to find the distance that other grandchildren had with their grandparents. But it wasn't possible to go back in time. The damage—the love—was already done.

SEVEN

Family of Four

1992

X

I was sleeping over at a friend's house when my mom's water broke. I spent the next day there, waiting to hear word of my new brother. At 9:00 PM, my dad called.

"He's here," he said triumphantly. I could hear my new brother crying in the background.

The following day, my dad picked me up and took me to the hospital to meet him. As I held my brother's small body on my lap, trying to figure him out—how he would fit into the family we had for the last ten years—a nurse came in the room.

"Do we have a name yet?" she asked.

"Not yet." My mom shook her head. "I'm not leaving until it's figured out," she told my dad.

"Fitzgibbon," my dad suggested. My mom and I looked at each other and laughed.

"Just let me know and I'll bring the paperwork in," the nurse said, fighting a laugh.

"That sounds like a monkey," my mom cried.

"That's terrible," I agreed. "Can I choose his middle name?"

"What do you want?" she asked.

"Daniel?"

"Okay, how about Jedd Daniel?" my mom tried. She'd been vying for the name Jedd for a while. My dad nodded, defeated, and I looked back down at my brother.

When we got home, now a family of four, I moved into the apartment's living room, with a raised bed handed down to me by my best friend. There was a sliding door underneath that opened up to storage space that I used as a clubhouse. A green Christmas bulb lit the dark space. My parents took the only bedroom with my newborn brother.

I was happy with my new sleeping arrangement. The storage space under the bed reminded me of the joy I found sitting in makeshift spaceships my dad had made for me as a kid. He'd construct them with cardboard boxes, cutting a hole through the front and standing them in the middle of the living room. When the TV was tuned to a snowy channel with the sound turned up, it had replicated space travel. I'd sit for hours in that box, the TV screaming at me, content with my private space.

That year in school, we read the book *Slake's Limbo,* about a boy who lived in a New York City subway tunnel. I'm sure it's meant to sadden readers, to draw their empathy and concern, but I read the book with enthusiasm. Slake's filthy version of a tree house sounded cozy and, to be honest, rejuvenating, like a remote cabin getaway. He had complete control over how many empty bottles or other found trinkets he wanted in his home. There was also complete privacy— aside from the few neighboring rats. But rats can't yell at you or hog the bathroom.

Despite the changes that came with my brother, I found that I was instantly in love with him. He so intrigued me that I would sneak into the bedroom while he was napping and gently pinch his thigh so that he would wake up. I was also keenly aware that now there would be four of us sharing the apartment. The bed in the living room was new and exciting at first, but with each passing day, I realized that it wasn't really my space.

With the new addition to our family, and the general insanity a newborn brings to a home—more so to a tiny apartment—I found myself in Daddy Joe's apartment more frequently. By the time I was twelve, I could take the bus downtown by myself.

"Siblings are great," Daddy Joe told me. "My kids had the best time together. Always getting into trouble."

I thought of my mom as a young kid, playing with her siblings.

"My mom said that Jimmy told her bees liked to be pet so that she would get stung."

Daddy Joe looked down into his coffee and thought for a moment. "I don't remember that. But we had an old boat on the property of the Stony Brook house. They used to play in it for hours." He shook his head, deep in thought. "Most kids have tree houses or something, but they had a boat. Can you imagine?"

I loved picturing a younger Daddy Joe. But I also couldn't help but feel a twinge of jealousy toward my mom for all the extra years she'd had with him. With the arrival of my brother, the idea of sharing became overwhelming. The place I slept, the living room, was shared with the whole family. The apartment was within a shared building. The building was within a shared city. Daddy Joe was a shared piece of my existence, too.

I became greedy about my time with him, grumpy when he had other people over at the same time. Sharing Daddy Joe was hard to do but also difficult to avoid. Some of the visitors I knew, and others were new and beaming, enthralled by his stories. From comic book collectors to friends such as Carmine Infantino, an artist from the Silver Age of Comic Books, there was a good chance that when I walked through his front door, I would find someone sitting on his red futon. I'd smile and say hello, trying my best not to mope at our interruption.

During one of these visits, a photographer was taking portraits of Daddy Joe. As an artist who retouched photos for newspapers in the beginning of his career, he knew the damage a glare on glass could cause, so he wore special lensless glasses. He liked to poke his finger through the empty lenses and laugh at his ingenuity.

"How's this?" he asked the photographer, angling himself in front of the first sketch of Captain America, the one that had been presented to Martin Goodman—before the round shield. The original angular shield made it to the first issue, but they were threatened with a lawsuit from MLJ Productions, a different comics publisher. They owned a character called the Shield whose costume design resembled the angular shield. Cap's shield was quickly changed to a circle.

"Great, Joe. That's great."

The photographer clicked the camera, and I watched from a chair near the kitchen.

"I'm not too ugly? Megan, am I too ugly?"

I smiled from the chair as he and the photographer laughed.

"Hey, why don't I get one with your granddaughter?" the photographer asked.

I perked up. "Really?"

Daddy Joe waved me over. I tightened my half ponytail and joined him. The camera lens was wide and slightly intimidating.

"Okay, Megan, why don't you put your arm around his shoulders," the photographer directed.

"You know, Megan is mine," Daddy Joe told him.

I put my arm on Daddy Joe's shoulder, feeling the warmth of his body against my forearm. I thought I could feel the blood running through his veins, his heart beating against my skin. It was as if we were one person, or that I was merely another part of him.

EIGHT

Growing Up

1994–1995

✕

We were almost at the East Side exit out of Central Park, my dad driving our old pea-green Saab, me in the front seat, when the car in front of us stopped abruptly.

"Fucking cocksucker!" my dad exclaimed while slamming on the brakes. I stared at him, my hand clutching the passenger-side door, startled by not only his words but also the bumpy ride. His driving was usually smooth and confident, likely to lull me to sleep. And then something occurred to me.

"I know what that means," I told him, grinning mischievously.

He looked at me, embarrassed, surely not thrilled that I knew what "cocksucker" meant, and nodded. "Okay," he said, looking back to the road ahead of us, unsure of what to do with that information.

It wouldn't be the first time I embarrassed my dad with my enthusiasm for growing up. Soon after that incident, I convinced my mom to buy me deodorant.

"I smell!" I insisted, sniffing each armpit.

I picked out the stick with the most obnoxious floral scent at the drugstore, and when I got home, I removed it from the paper bag and approached my dad, who was watching the PBS NewsHour with his dinner on a lap tray. I rested my forearms on his chair, my knees on the wood floor.

"Look what I got," I said, holding up the deodorant like a medal. He nodded, avoiding eye contact.

These milestones felt few and far between. It was taking forever to grow up. The other girls in my class were all a head taller than me, and my flat chest was unattractive and boring next to their newly curved bodies. Boys rolled their pencils off their desks and asked the voluptuous girls to pick them up for them. I sat back. I wasn't stupid. I knew they had no interest in watching me bend over for anything.

My aunt Gail tried to comfort me. "Your mother and I took a long time to develop, too. Harriet told us, 'The fruit that takes longest to ripen is always the sweetest.'"

My turn came when I was fourteen, during a sleepover at my best friend Ro's apartment. Ro lived across the street in a building with hundreds of windows that looked like the pockets of a waffle. She had her own room, where clothes often piled into mountains that we used for back support as we watched TV. I woke up in the morning to pee and found spots of reddish-brown in my underwear. I knew what was happening. How could I not? I was officially the last girl in my class to get my period. I'd been waiting impatiently for almost a year.

I was relieved and disgusted. Ro squealed for me, and then told her mom, who clapped her hands together and hugged me. I asked to use the phone to call my mom.

"Mom."

"Megan?"

"Yeah, guess what?"

"You got your period."

"How did you know?" I asked, annoyed with her psychic abilities.

"I just knew. Plus, you were acting crazy the past few days."

"Oh."

"What time are you coming home?"

"I don't know, why?"

"Can you watch Jedd for me?"

I couldn't believe it. Was this all she cared about? What time her live-in babysitter would be home? How was it that Ro's mom was more excited about my becoming a woman? Wasn't this a big deal in a girl's life? In a daughter's life?

"Mom," I whined. "I just watched him yesterday."

"I'll give you ten bucks."

I exhaled loudly. "Fine. I'm going to need pads or something."

"I'll pick them up when I'm out. Can you be home by one?"

Ж

Although I had eagerly awaited puberty, when the hormone surge finally hit, it bowled me over. I wasn't prepared for the desperate need for privacy—the apartment wasn't prepared for me, either. I was moved again, back to the only bedroom, though now I shared it with my brother, our headboards touching. My parents took the living room back for themselves.

These were the years in which most teenagers were figuring out who they were—taping photos of friends to their walls, hiding out in their bedrooms to make prank phone calls, and giggling over yearbook photos. I was convinced that there was a teenage life out there that was better than my own. Large high schools with long, bright hallways lined with lockers, and expansive football fields. I daydreamed about driving with friends, the windows rolled down, doing that wavy-hand thing in the wind like I'd seen in a Smashing Pumpkins video; spending nights in my own bedroom, the sounds of crickets coming in through a window, a lamp delicately illuminating homework, a soft knock on the door: "Dinner's ready."

I thought life in the suburbs was the ultimate, storybook, John Hughes mecca.

Meanwhile, in apartment 1K, I was far from a John Hughes movie. Even though I had a little nook, I didn't dare decorate the walls around my bed. The last time I'd had any say in what was put on the walls had been when I was seven and my mom framed my drawing of a farm. It hung on the bathroom wall, a straight view from the toilet.

I became desperate to find some space that was solely mine, and noticed more and more how the apartment belonged to my mom. There were dried flowers, representing the house and garden that she yearned for, and seashells and beach glass sprinkled on the windowsills. Old rusted lanterns, similar to the ones her mother collected when she was younger, hung on the apartment walls. The built-in bookshelves in the dining room/foyer displayed handmade bowls and a clay castle with a fitted top that held receipts and important documents. On the bottom shelf, about fifteen corn-husk dolls stood like an army, holding gardening tools made from twigs and wearing long, yellow husk skirts with cloth aprons and bonnets. Whenever I tried to play with them as a kid she'd yell, "Don't break them!" These were her toys and not mine.

My mom's closet was also off-limits. It sat across from my dad's closet, both of them by the apartment's front door. The top shelf was filled with old radios, answering machines, mints, and gum. Whenever I got a craving for something sweet, I waited until my mom was out of the apartment, pulled up a chair to the edge of the closet, and searched under folded sweaters and towels for Mentos or Pep O Mint Lifesavers. I prayed that she wouldn't walk in the door and catch me, but she was so aware of her things that the slightest wrinkle in her towels tipped her off to my snooping.

Once as a kid, while my mom was in the bathroom, I pulled a tube of lipstick from the top shelf of her closet. I applied it, looking in the mirror nailed to the inside of the closet door, checking behind me to make sure the bathroom door hadn't opened. And then I took nibble of it, the lipstick mashing between my teeth, a soft, dusty taste to it. I heard the toilet flush in the bathroom, used a tissue to remove the evidence from my lips and teeth, and placed it back on the shelf, looking as if a mouse had gotten to it. Later, when she asked me if I knew what had happened to her lipstick, I pleaded ignorance.

Perhaps my bad habit of picking my nose and hiding my findings on the wall next to my bed was an attempt to mark my territory. My mom informed me years later that she found these artifacts grasping the walls for dear life, much like the goldfish we thought had been eaten by the cat but was actually dried on the wall behind the dresser. It was embarrassing to be called out, but at least my message of "I live here, too" was heard loud and clear.

Luckily for me, our new computer was kept in the bedroom. I had gotten it for Hanukkah that year for typing up homework assignments, instead of using Daddy Joe's electric typewriter, which vigorously slapped the paper with each letter.

I also discovered AOL chat rooms and waited for everyone to go to sleep to embark on my online adventures. As my little brother lay across the room, I booted up my Apple IIe and connected to AOL, the dial-up connection trilling under my hand as I tried to muffle the speaker's sound. Once, while trying to plug in the computer in the dark bedroom, my fingers slipped between the outlet and the plug, sending a sharp current of electricity up my arm. I kept my yelp sealed behind my lips.

"You've got mail," the computer sang, and then came the ping of my current online boyfriend welcoming my arrival with a *what's up?* It was my dirty little secret, hunched over the keyboard, my parents settling in for bed and my little brother probably dreaming of Hess trucks behind me.

You should send me a photo in the mail, the online stranger suggested after weeks of chatting. He lived in New Jersey, not too far, so I held hope that if he liked my photo and things continued to go well, we would meet in person and fall in love, my boyfriend hunt—and my life—complete. With a promise from him of returning the favor, I put a photo from a school dance, me in a tight silver dress, into an envelope. I waited days, weeks, and then months for word from him—a positive reaction to my photo, or a photo of his own. No word came, and the AOL chat rooms quickly lost their appeal.

As I got older, I got angrier. Why didn't my parents understand my need to claim space, *any space*, in our apartment? Why did they think I was so unreasonable? My tantrums quickly escalated from moping around the house to more destructive behavior. The anger startled me.

Only six years earlier, I had been thrilled by games of entrapment, my dad chasing me around the apartment, grunting like a hungry bear. If I was caught, my mission was to hold as still as possible so that the bear wouldn't eat me up. All it took were a few sniffs and grunts to set me off in hysterics, failing the game miserably.

Our other game was called the "Daddy Trap." Locked beneath my dad, who was on all fours, I had to find a way to escape as he sang, "Megan's stuck in the Daddy trap!"

I was so fearless and lacking in anxiety as a child. Roller coasters and other spinning carnival rides thrilled me. Even being trapped left me giggling. But now all I wanted was a door to close behind me or a wall on which to tape up photos of friends. The closest I came to decorating was to carve the word "bitch" with a pen into the wooden nightstand that divided my bed from my brother's.

I've really lost it, I thought to myself as I first dug the pen into the wood. I had been crying after another fight with my mom, my head against my pillow, my brother's bed adjacent to my headboard. My mom was muttering to herself outside the bedroom, taking out her anger on the kitchen trash bag. I heard the slam of the apartment door, then the groan of the incinerator door out in the hallway. I found myself grabbing the pen and stabbing the bedside table. My hand pressed down, slowly and firmly, the soft wood bearing the brunt of our fight. I finished carving the "*H*" and admired my work. The letters were sharp and angled. I felt better already.

I left my anger in the apartment, in the grooves of the carved letters of the nightstand, and headed downtown to Daddy Joe's. We walked together to CVS, my life uptown almost, though not quite, forgotten. I focused on matching the strides of his long legs and the pauses to look at signs on lampposts. They were probably an excuse for him to rest for a moment, and I read them, too, pretending not to suspect such a thing.

As we walked through the automatic doors of CVS, Daddy Joe paused at the plastic shopping baskets and looked around. "I'll be in the toothpaste aisle," he concluded. "Get whatever you want."

We parted ways, and I went in search of press-on nails and lip gloss—things that would make me feel not only grown up but also beautiful. After I got my period, I gained about ten pounds, though I hadn't noticed it, or I guess I didn't care, until my physical that year.

"Why don't you try eating more salad?" the doctor had suggested, and my mom nodded in the corner of the room. I had pretended it was an idea I was interested in trying.

I was struggling with finding a place to feel welcome, to be comfortable in my own skin. A place to sit alone and unpack everything that was changing in my life. I was desperate to claim something—a room, a wall, even my body.

I spotted the hair dye and ran my finger down the boxes of lush-haired models. I decided that my light brown hair needed a boost. I saw the jet-black dye and thought how darker hair would help my blue eyes pop.

"Megan?" I heard Daddy Joe yelling across the store. "Where's the goddamned toothpaste? Megan?"

I grabbed the box of dye and hurried to find him before he made more of a scene. Daddy Joe was tapping an employee on the shoulder, the employee holding up his finger to him.

"Sir, just a moment," he said, walking away, irritated by the interruption.

"Go ahead, I don't want you to be late for charm school," Daddy Joe said, grinning at the man's back.

After finding the toothpaste, we headed to the checkout. I was nervous Daddy Joe would see the box of dye and question my purchase, but he simply handed me his credit card and waited by the door.

That night, I waited for my parents to finish putting my brother to bed before I took over the bathroom for a shower. The sink was decorated with black spatter by the time I finished rubbing all the dye into my hair. I looked at my reflection in the mirror and felt a twinge of regret. My skin was already stained around my forehead and ears, no matter how hard I scrubbed with the washcloth. I started the shower, deciding that was enough time, even if the box called for another five minutes.

I was almost finished blow drying my hair when my mom walked in.

"I need to brush my—" she began. "Oh, fuck! Megan!"

I pretended I was pleased with the result, but I looked like Wednesday Addams's chubby sister. The only thing the black hair did for my eyes was accentuate the dark circles under them.

"Papa!" she whisper-screamed to my dad, so that she wouldn't wake my brother. "Look what she did!"

I pushed past her and slithered into the dark bedroom before he could see me. I didn't want to deal with their reactions or their judgment.

The new hair had felt like a mistake the moment I put the dye on my head, but that wasn't the point—I was claiming something as my own. I could decorate my body however I wanted. It was the one thing that was mine. This new control I had would be the perfect way to start high school.

NINE

Distractions

1995–1996

XX

"Hi, baby. How's school going?" Daddy Joe asked me as I peeled the skin off the mashed potatoes of my microwavable meal. It was 11:30 in the morning, and he had just woken up.

"Okay, I guess."

The truth was, I didn't want to talk about it. It had only been a week since I started high school, and I had yet to make any real friends. I spent each lunch period in his apartment heating up a Hungry-Man meal.

Daddy Joe turned on the coffeemaker and waited for the gurgle. "You'll make friends soon enough."

I shrugged, even though his back was to me.

Daddy Joe sat at his kitchen table, reading the paper with his coffee, and when I was done eating, I tossed the plastic container, viscous gravy hanging off it, into the trash and headed for the door. My stomach was sour from the crappy lunch and the thought of the next few hours sitting under the fluorescent lights of my new classrooms.

A month into the new school year, I finally made friends, and instead of walking to Daddy Joe's apartment during lunch, I hid in the concrete tunnels of the local projects' playground. My new friends and I, each of our bodies curved into a C-shape to fit, lit the tops of our tiny bowls—glass pipes with swirls of blue and green and filled with weed—and watched the smoke escaping from either side of the tunnel like a smoldering cannoli.

Sometimes we skipped class to roam the aisles of the nearby Tower Records on Broadway. I eyed the new box set of the Smashing Pumpkins' *Mellon Collie and the Infinite Sadness*. As I dragged my finger across the clear plastic wrapping, holding the two disc sets together, Chloe, a new friend, nudged my shoulder. She had mastered the look of not giving a fuck. Her hair was long, black, curly, and disheveled. She wore baggy T-shirts and wide-legged raver pants—she had stolen many times.

"Just take it," she whispered.

"It's huge!" I said out of the side of my mouth.

"Just put it under your sweatshirt," she whispered again, pointing her chin toward my baggy clothes.

It felt like a test. Would I be able to hang with my new friends, or would I be banished to Hungry-Man meals for the rest of my high school career? I thought of the frozen meal, the skin of the mashed potatoes that I liked to pull off the top and eat, Daddy Joe's eyes on me, probably wondering why I didn't have a social life. I put the box set under my sweatshirt.

I was not built, genetically, to be a bad girl. My nervous system was built by anxious Russian Jews with bad stomachs. I was created to hunker down in a warm, but not too warm, home while sipping chicken broth. My legs felt weak beneath me, and stomach acid rose to the back of my throat as I walked out the door of Tower Records. Outside in the cool early-winter air, successful in my mission, I thanked god for letting me survive my first, and probably last, theft.

To avoid getting in trouble for skipping class, I usually called my mom from a pay phone to whimper that I didn't feel well.

"I just wanted to sit outside and get some air," I'd lie.

Easier than skipping class was filling plastic running bottles with vodka and sipping during Spanish class, while Mr. Sendorowitz spoke in fast, fluent Spanish. He paced in front of the chalkboard, wearing winter boots that looked appropriate for a moon expedition. Four of us passed the bottle around discreetly, trying to keep up the facade of being deeply interested in his español.

During a bathroom escape from class, I found a girl named Becky, with her snaggletoothed grin and gold chains, smoking a cigarette. We weren't friends ourselves, but with our mutual friends, I was comfortable giving her a small, "Hey."

"Want one?" she asked, holding out a pack of Virginia Slims.

"Sure." I took one and lit it with her cigarette. I had just started this new habit, another attempt to fit in, to take control. I had even brought a cigarette home from school to give to my best friend, Ro, who was having trouble finding one to try in Catholic school. We smoked it on the playground behind her building.

I was already buzzed from the vodka, so the first two drags of the cigarette left me light-headed and queasy. Luckily, after swinging her long strawberry blond hair around her shoulder, Becky threw hers into the toilet.

"I should get back," she said while washing her hands.

"Yeah, me too," I said, relieved.

X

Sometimes my friends and I rambled our way to Sheep's Meadow in Central Park, our wide-legged jeans dragging as we walked, the ends frayed and wet. We spent the early-evening hours enjoying the seemingly endless landscape, the sun still hovering over the West Side's buildings. We lounged on the grass and smoked thin joints behind the few trees outlining the field—tumbling, cartwheeling, legs reaching clumsily to the sky.

The rest of the city began to pack up and leave as the sun made its final descent, but we weren't ready to go. We had nowhere else to head but home, and the vastness of the meadow was still too delicious. We continued our escapades uninterrupted for a few hours, the sky growing darker, the buildings shining brighter.

"Cops!" my friend Andy yelled. We hit the ground as if we'd fallen from the sky without parachutes.

"Can they see us?" I asked into the dirt, the grass tickling my nostrils. I didn't dare lift my head.

"I have no idea," I heard someone answer, muffled. "Keep your head down and they won't see us."

"Park's closed!" a cop yelled from beyond the wire fence, at least two hundred feet from us. It was dark enough and we were stoned enough to believe we were invisible.

I turned my head so that my left ear pressed against the ground and I could see the skyline of the buildings of Central Park South, buildings that were meant for a different breed of people—the wealthy New Yorkers. I thought of Daddy Joe south of us, watching *The Simpsons* in his apartment. Beyond the faint sounds of traffic outside the park, the glow of the buildings eased softly into the dark sky. Andy broke the silence with a fart noise against the damp ground.

"You think they're gone?" I asked. Just then a spotlight from a cop car danced across the dark meadow, bouncing against our flat bodies.

"We see you," the cop said, bored, through a speaker. "Let's go."

A collective groan vibrated among us, and we slowly got up, pulling our messenger bags onto our shoulders. Defeated, the pack of us headed west, out of the park, onto the streets, and back uptown.

TEN

Family of Five

1998

※

My mom was on the futon in the living room, propped up with a few large pillows. Her hand rested on her large pregnant stomach, her eyes closed. I plopped down beside her, and she looked at me.

"Want to feel her move? Her foot is trying to push through." My mom lifted her shirt to reveal the imprint of a small foot.

I placed my hand on the small mound rising from my mom's stomach. "Ew," I said. "Does that hurt?"

My mom shook her head and closed her eyes again.

"Did I move around this much? When I was in your stomach?"

She opened her eyes again, looking toward the kitchen, where my dad was using every pot available in the kitchen to make dinner. My brother was enjoying an episode of *Barney & Friends*.

"I don't remember," she said. "I just remember how sick you made me in the beginning."

My mom, now forty-one, was eight months pregnant with my sister. Just like when my brother was conceived, I was totally blindsided, assuming that the ship had sailed, that we were bound to be a family of four.

But when I found out this time, I was furious, screaming, "Why can't you just keep your pants on?!"

How could they be so irresponsible, bringing another human into these already tight living quarters? This of course was a concern to my parents, too, but what was most important to them was grasping the opportunity to raise another child—no matter how many bedrooms we had. What was important to me, a hormonal teenager, was privacy. I hadn't given birth. I hadn't lived the thrill of bringing a child into the world, loving it, and raising it to be someone to be proud of. I was simply a trapped animal.

As my mom's stomach grew, her hormones reached epic heights alongside mine. I was almost seventeen, and entering that stage of my life where everything meant too much. I needed the space to feel all of these things, a place to put them down for a moment, breathe, recollect myself. But there wasn't enough room for things like that, especially when my mom was carrying her own literal and metaphorical weight. Watching my sister's foot knead against the wall of my mom's stomach, I could feel the apartment getting smaller.

✕

The day my mom went into labor, I stayed home with my brother. I fed him dinner, bathed him, and got him ready for bed.

"When is Mommy and Daddy gonna be home?" he asked from under his blankets.

"In a couple of days, but we're going to see them in the morning. We're going to the hospital to meet our new sister. Are you excited?"

He nodded, unsure what it all meant.

Back in the living room, I lay beneath my parents' blankets watching a *Friends* rerun. During a commercial, I scanned the apartment. My brother asleep, the distant sounds of the occasional siren from the street, the hum of the fridge. I knew that when my parents returned home, the apartment would become even more of a challenge for me. I wondered how I would fit—not just physically, but within my parents' radar. I had the SATs and college on my horizon. Would I be on my own? I couldn't help but feel I was instantaneously an adult, left to my own devices with these huge life decisions. My parents needed what little time and energy they had for their newborn and six-year-old son. I was now seventeen—capable of taking care of myself.

The next morning, after a breakfast of Special K, my brother and I hopped in a cab and headed across the park to Mount Sinai Hospital on the East Side. Walking into the hospital room, I saw my parents as a stranger might—as new parents. I saw them seventeen years earlier, experiencing their first birth. They were both tired but renewed.

After my brother was born, I was away that summer at farm camp in the Catskills, and my dad sent me a letter about the joys of having children. It was written on a plain white piece of paper, with a thick drawing pencil. "I feel like a different person these days," he wrote. "One of the wonderful things about having children, as you will one day find out for yourself, is that in their birth you are reborn yourself. . . . Everything is fresh, new, and possible."

I didn't feel that sense of renewal or hope when I held my new sister, who my parents named Jillian, swaddled in a white receiving blanket. Even with the task of giving her a middle name (I chose Leah), I was oddly separated from the situation, as if I was a ghost from the past, watching this new family begin.

✕

"I think we should put up a sliding door or something, so I can have some privacy," I informed my parents a few weeks after they returned from the hospital.

My mom threw her hands over her head. "So we have to sleep in the bedroom with two children? You're not the only one who wants privacy—we're a married couple!"

"Yeah, well, who keeps having kids in this tiny apartment?" I hissed.

My mother laughed at my gall. "Fine, it's only for another year, until you go to college." She looked at my dad. "Papa, what do you think?"

My dad wasn't listening. "How about we build a sort of bunk bed contraption, but instead of beds on top of each other, there would be a wall of pods with little doors?"

My mom and I looked at each other.

"You know," he continued, "you could have your privacy once the door was pulled down." His eyes gleamed with creative genius, much like the spark in his eye when working with the old cardboard boxes. His cardboard spaceships had been fun; sleeping in pods was another thing.

My parents ended up building a sliding glass door at the far end of the living room to form a little space for my bed, bookshelf, and bureau. It wasn't a John Hughes movie existence, but it was an improvement.

ELEVEN

Always Back to Him

1998

⋈

My friends and I pushed our way to the front of the crowd at Roseland Ballroom. Alanis Morissette came out on stage, only five feet from our faces, her long hair waving like a flag, and we were transported far away from our apartments and the busy streets of the city. We knew all the words. We screamed the lyrics, releasing every frustration, every disappointment up to the ceiling.

After a sweaty Alanis left the stage, her black leather pants receding out of sight, we filed out through the lobby with the rest of the crowd. To stay together, we hooked our fingers, aware we were almost outside by only the scent of the fresh air mixed with cigarette smoke. Outside, we pulled out boxes of Parliament Lights, some of my friends preferring the throat burn of Marlboro Reds. We inhaled hard, still buzzing from the lyrics and blue lights. This was before crowds made me want to climb the walls, when I was only grateful for the escape.

We walked uptown toward the subway, annoying others on the sidewalk with our yelps and squeals in the way that only high school kids can. *Fuck everyone else, this is our city.* We knew the majority of adults who avoided our cluster of noise were transplants, not natives like us. We loved the power and importance that this fact brought us.

"Hold up," I said. "I need to use the phone."

We were only five blocks from Daddy Joe's apartment and I wasn't ready to head home. As much as I relied on my friends and our outings, the lure of Daddy Joe's, the promise of his sweet cigar smoke and the white noise of his TV, was too strong to ignore. No matter how exhilarating my night out was, I found myself wanting to walk through his door, hear the clank of it behind me, to enter the warmth of his small apartment.

I dialed his phone number, holding the receiver of the pay phone close enough so that I could hear, but far enough away that I couldn't catch syphilis of the ear.

"Hello?" His voice radiated with its usual bravado.

"Hi, Daddy Joe. It's Megan. Can I come over?"

"Sure! Come on up. You can tell me what you think of this character, Jove. He'll solve problems by instruction or destruction."

I laughed. "Okay. Be there in ten."

I hung up and dialed again, this time my parents' number. The answering machine picked up, but before I could leave a message my mom's voice broke through.

"Hello," she mumbled into the phone. I pictured her curls wild and her long flannel pajama pants tucked under her heels from shuffling sleepily to the phone. I knew the apartment was dark, my dad, brother, and newborn sister asleep in the bedroom.

"Hi," I said. "I'm going to sleep at Daddy Joe's."

Someone asked for a cigarette behind me and was quickly shushed by the group for their mistake of letting a parent hear them. But my mom was too tired to hear or care.

"Okay," she mumbled again. And then came the whining of my newborn sister, born at almost ten pounds and growing fast, her size marking her territory in the apartment. My mom seemed to wake up in that instant. "Okay," she said again with a hint of irritation.

"Bye."

I heard the click of the receiver. I knew one less person in the apartment for the night was a relief for her.

I parted ways with my friends at Fifty-Sixth Street and Eighth Avenue with a kiss on each of their cheeks and a wave. Walking down the dark block toward Daddy Joe's building, I watched how red brick ascended from the concrete to form the wall of the front courtyard of his building. I remembered running up that narrow slope as a child, nothing but thick bangs and knobby knees, racing him to the building's entrance, a sliding glass door with a doorman behind a desk greeting us.

His apartment glowed from the five lamps placed around the living room. It was almost eleven by then, and his cigar had been lit, the sliding window cracked open to let the smoke snake its way out. Rush Limbaugh's ranting carried through the apartment from his bedroom tape cassette player. If I didn't listen to the words, I found comfort in the noise. It was familiar, his bad taste in talk radio, and the effort to not say anything about it.

"Hi, baby. You can have the bedroom if you want."

"That's okay, I don't mind sleeping out here." I sat on the red futon that would be my bed that night.

"I'm going to be up for a while." The cigar rested between his fingers. He looked like a relaxed mobster making a deal. "Are you hungry? I made some soup. There's new farfel above the desk."

I shook my head. "Not hungry."

"How was the concert? Was it fun?"

"Yeah."

"*Yes*," he corrected me with a grin.

I rolled my eyes and headed to his room to fish through his drawers for a T-shirt and boxer shorts to wear to bed. Daddy Joe was over six feet tall, so his shirts reached my knees.

Even after taking a quick shower in the tub that smelled like hot chalk, I was still wound up from the concert and cigarettes. Daddy

Joe hadn't moved—still in his brown chair, and still nursing the cigar. I scanned the bookshelf for his photo albums and took one down.

"I like this photo," I said. My finger rested on one of Harriet crossing her legs as she watched Daddy Joe work at his tilted art table, one much like the table sitting in the middle of his apartment.

"She used to sit with me for hours," he said. "When she was angry with the twins, they would hide under the table."

"Why? What would she do?"

"Used to chase them around with a broom," he said, and laughed, his chin to the air.

My mom told me that the only time she remembered Daddy Joe getting angry with her was when, annoyed with his loud chewing at the breakfast table, she'd built a wall with the cereal boxes between them. "Cut it out!" he'd hollered, knocking over the boxes.

I couldn't imagine Daddy Joe being the disciplinarian. "You never punished them?" I asked.

"No, I was cool, man. When the twins were teenagers, they started a garden right under my studio window. I thought it was so nice that they were into gardening." He laughed again. "I used to drop the ash from my cigars out the window, right onto their garden, and I think that helped because the plants were huge, up to here." He held his hands four or five feet from his parquet floors.

"What were they growing?"

"Well, wait, listen. I asked them, and they told me tomatoes or something, and I'm a moron and didn't think twice even though there wasn't ever fruit on the things. One morning we wake up and their garden is totally gone. Plants disappeared." He paused for dramatic effect. "It was pot, and the guy who delivered the heating oil stole it."

I loved hearing stories about my mom misbehaving. It made me feel better about the minor infractions I was committing. "Did you ever smoke with them?" I asked.

"Once," he said matter-of-factly. "I didn't feel anything." (Later, I asked my mom, and she debunked this. "We couldn't keep him out of the fridge!" she exclaimed.)

Looking through the photo albums that night, listening to his stories of a life before me, I tried to imagine being my mom. Playing house in an old boat in their Long Island yard, eating the five-pound lobsters Daddy Joe surprised the family with at least once every few months. "Enjoy Florida," he used to say before dropping them in the pot—he said the same thing to the one-pound supermarket lobsters we bought together.

They'd lived in a few houses over the years. Harriet liked to buy them, fix them up, sell them for more money, and then move on to the next project. When Harriet's father died, her mother, Dinah, announced that she was going to come live with Daddy Joe, Harriet, and their five children. Harriet started looking for bigger houses and landed on a mansion in Stony Brook built by a famous pianist who was friendly with the Rockefellers. The house sat on a cliff overlooking the Long Island Sound and had a clear view to Fairfield, Connecticut. It boasted eight bathrooms, as well as a horse barn that had been converted to a guest house.

Dinah ended up not moving in, after all that. "She was annoying in many ways, but she was a good woman," Daddy Joe said.

Looking at photos of that house, I saw privilege, a life that I could only dream of.

"At least you have a family," my mom often shot back. "I had the huge house, but not the family."

For them, that mansion came to represent a place of heartache and loss.

One of my favorite photos was enlarged and printed with the help of Daddy Joe's copy machine. He had taped the black-and-white print on the metal filing cabinet that separated his living room from the front door. In it, Harriet was brushing her hair, looking in the bathroom mirror, wearing only a shirt, underwear, ankle socks, and loafers.

Her bangs were flipped in a 1950s curl, the rest of her hair curling toward the nape of her neck.

"She was so cute," Daddy Joe said once, when I asked him about the photo.

My mom didn't talk about her mother a lot. There were tidbits of information that I collected and filed away to try to solve the puzzle of her life at a later date. I knew that Harriet had a sister, Dottie, who had the same high cheekbones as me, and a brother, Arnold, who, to their mother's dismay, married a German woman. I knew that Harriet worshipped the sun, so much so that Daddy Joe built a little area off the side of their house with walls and no roof so that she could sunbathe in the nude.

"She was always lying in the sun, couldn't get enough." He thought for a moment, then, looking beyond my shoulder, added, "It probably wasn't good for her."

X

At 2:00 AM, in the darkness, the familiar sounds of Daddy Joe's apartment seemed to vibrate—the hard clicks of his three clocks, his snoring from the bedroom on the other side of the wall. I was pretty sure I heard a mouse scurry in the kitchen, most likely with a piece of fallen chocolate tucked in its cheek.

Even though I'd showered when I'd arrived a few hours before—an attempt to wash the smell of fruity beer and cigarettes from my body—I could still smell smoke on my fingertips. The sounds of the concert still echoed in my head. Trying to get comfortable on the stiff red futon, I rolled over to face the windows, Daddy Joe's large T-shirt twisting around my waist. The lights of the city aggressively pushed their way through the sides of the blinds, giving his drawing table a luminous glow. Captain America hung above my head, reaching toward me with his shield.

TWELVE

Claiming New York

1998

Ж

After fights with my parents, I called Ro to ask if she wanted to take a walk. Our other friends were summoned, and we each left our apartments, some of them bigger than others, most of them bursting with our teenaged frustrations, and met at the Monument. Dark, breezy, and secluded, it was ours. We could smoke our Parliament Lights freely, our laughs bouncing off the stone and the smoke reaching widely to the sky.

The Monument, more formally known as the Soldiers' and Sailors' Monument, on Eighty-Ninth Street and Riverside Drive, was secluded at night, with only a few people walking past with their dogs—and maybe an occasional drive-by from the police to make sure we were behaving and not climbing the large gray structure. Once, Ro, in her white patent platform sandals, and I scaled the ledge of the Monument and hoisted ourselves up on top of the eagle statue. I pretended to ride him, light-headed from the climb and the height.

One Saturday night, as we walked from the Monument up to Broadway, we heard a *thwap-thwap* somewhere ahead of us.

"What's that noise?" I asked Ro.

Before she could answer, I locked eyes with a man crouched behind a black garbage bin in the small courtyard of a brownstone, maybe twenty feet from us. Ro and I screamed as though there were hundreds of cockroaches crawling all over our bodies. He ran, sprinting toward a bike that he hopped onto in one swift move, and peddled himself and his hard-on toward West End Avenue.

Like most things in the city, the Monument wasn't just ours. Bike Guy became something of a regular during our nights there. Although he still caught us on our walks up to Broadway, mostly between parked cars, he preferred to hide in the bushes that bordered the white stone of the Monument and the path leading to the Hudson River walkway.

Weeks after his first appearance behind the trash can, we were now so accustomed to the interruptions that when one of us spotted him crouched behind a bush, the familiar *thwap-thwap* sounds carried by the Hudson River's wind, we'd yell, "Ah, come on! Get out of here!" How dare he intrude our sacred place. As all of us stood and screamed in annoyance, he'd escape on his old blue bike, sufficiently shaken up and turned on.

There were three places to gather at the Monument. The first was a set of wooden benches, each with their own marble chess table, which was usually used for rolling joints or blunts that we all greedily eyed. The second was the large Monument itself, with its carved, circular stone bench underneath the eagle. My favorite spot was where the flagpole stood, a small inlet set against the trees outlining the path down to the Hudson. There was a stone bench carved in this spot as well, but I usually opted to sit on the ledge of the wall. Up there, I could feel the rush of the wind, hear the rustle of the blowing trees. Up there, I was far away from the city and close to the sky.

One evening, my legs straddling the ledge, a twenty-foot drop to my left, I looked at the treetops and sighed. "I can't wait to get out of there," I said to Ro. I took a drag off my cigarette and released the smoke in one slow exhale. Ro was an only child with her own bedroom, but she had known me since I was six months old. She understood the family dynamic that rumbled within my one-bedroom apartment.

"One more year," she told me. We both knew that she would never leave New York. I was going to escape like a convict, and she would settle in for the long haul.

X

One sunny spring day, Ro, our friend Connor, and I paid the Monument a rare daytime visit. It sprung to life in the daylight hours, morphing into something not quite ours. We decided to smoke the joint stashed in Connor's leather wallet, which was attached to his pants with a long, skater-appropriate chain. I never liked smoking during the day. Being high felt enjoyable only under the cover of night. But I also wasn't one to pass up free weed.

We sat on the backside of the Monument, hoping to avoid the attention of the families walking below on the sidewalk of Riverside Drive. We pulled, we exhaled, we watched the smoke smudge against the light sneaking through the mature trees.

"I'm done," I said, waving away the stub of a joint Connor held out to me. I was starting to feel too heavy for the sunshine. He pulled off it again and threw it behind the stone railing while jumping up onto his Rollerblades. After a slow, gliding circle, he built up speed and jumped to grind across the already worn-down stone of the bench. Ro and I watched him, giggling when he wavered and fell back on his ass.

"I have to get going," Connor told us, brushing dirt off the back of his baggy jeans. "I'm having lunch with my dad."

"I guess we'll head uptown, too. I have to pee." I peeled myself off the cool stone.

"My parents are going to a show tonight," Ro told me. "Want to come over?" Ro's dad wrote for a theater magazine, which meant that her parents were out most weekend nights, taking in the latest Broadway show. As an only child, this left Ro with the apartment to herself, and we usually took advantage by broiling chicken wings for dinner, dipping them in a vinegar and salt concoction, and smoking cigarettes out of her fifteenth-floor window while listening to Bush's "Glycerine."

We made our way to Broadway and then headed north, weaving around people, Connor making old women nervous with his quick turns and grinding breaks. I tried to squash the paranoid feeling that everyone was staring at me.

"I can't go home yet," I told Ro. "I'm way too high."

"Want to use the bathroom at my place and then go to the back-yard?" she asked. Her backyard was a concrete strip in the back of her building.

"Let's stop at the bodega first and get something to drink, and maybe some chips. Doritos!"

The three of us stopped on the corner of West Ninety-Sixth and Broadway, waiting for the walk light to head up to Amsterdam Avenue.

"Oh my god," Ro said, pinching my arm.

"Ow, what?"

"Isn't that your mom?" Connor asked.

Waiting for the light to change on the other side of Broadway was my mom, my six-year-old brother, and Daddy Joe. Before we could turn, my mom spotted me and pointed.

"Shit. Shit. Shit," I whispered.

We met in the island next to the subway station entrance. Ro turned red and silent. Connor grinned.

"Hi, baby!" Daddy Joe sang.

"What are you guys doing?" my mom asked. She was holding Jedd's hand, and he looked up at me with his brown eyes, a halo of brown curls atop his head.

I looked down to my worn green Vans. "Uh, just went for a walk," I said, thanking the heavens that I'd used Connor's eye drops before leaving the Monument.

"Megan," Daddy Joe continued. "What's Korn?"

"*Porn?*" I blurted. Everyone looked at me confused. "Did you just say porn?" I tried again, attempting a more casual approach.

"Your T-shirt," he said, he and my mom looking at each other with questioning smiles. "What does Korn mean?"

"Oh." I looked down at my shirt. Korn was a heavy metal band with only one song that I liked, but I felt like a badass wearing their shirt. "It's a band. Okay, I'm going to Ro's house. Bye."

My friends and I hurried on.

⋊⋉

Later that night, I unlocked my apartment door, praying that everyone was asleep, but I found my mom rustling around in the kitchen in her flannel pajamas. The apartment was dark except for the kitchen light, everyone else asleep in the bedroom. I closed the door, turned the bolt, hooked the chain, and turned back around to find her directly behind me.

"Where were you?" she asked, smiling.

"Mom, stop! Get out of my face!"

I tried to shoulder my way around her, but the foyer was too tight and she angled herself, keeping me close and as uncomfortable as possible. She knew I was paranoid about the cigarette smell and was joyously tormenting me. After months of "My sleeve smells because I was holding a cigarette for Rachel," my parents caught on to my secret habit.

"Did you have fun?" she continued, trying to keep a straight face.

"Yes. I'm taking a shower."

Her face shifted back to its usual look of annoyance. "Don't go in yet, I need the bathroom first," she said, breaking out of her game of entrapment.

"Then, go!" I said, breaking free and heading for my space behind the sliding glass doors in the living room. I ripped off my socks and sat on the edge of my bed, waiting to hear the flush of the toilet before heading to the shower.

A few months earlier, my mom had hammered a dinky hook-and-eye latch on the bathroom door. I loved the act of latching it, embracing the chance for some solitude—a door to lock behind me was precious.

After removing my smoky clothing, I stepped into the shower, angling my face up to the ferocious water pressure. Soon I lay down in the tub, allowing the water to beat against my body. I closed my eyes, relishing the white noise and the warmth of the steam.

Figuring everyone was asleep, I took my time, lying there for ten minutes until I heard the door handle rattle, the hook-and-eye latch shake. *Bang, bang, bang.*

"I need to get in there," I heard my mom whine from the other side of the door. "You've been in there for an hour!" *Bang, bang, bang.*

Peering from behind the shower curtain, I watched the hook begin to wiggle its way out of the wood of the jamb with each shove of the door. The steam began to feel oppressive, the apartment unbearable again.

THIRTEEN

San Diego Comic-Con

1998

)(

I hated flying, but most of all, I hated takeoff, when my whole world seemed to hang in limbo. Fear gathered in my limbs with each foot climbed. As I squeezed the armrests, willing the plane to safely make its ascent, Daddy Joe reached his hand out to mine, giving it a reassuring squeeze.

"It's okay," he said with a smile. "It's cool, man."

I loosened my grip from the armrest and reattached my hand to his, squeezing his long fingers. He laughed, but I knew I was making him nervous. His grin wasn't convincing me of anything—I knew he was also praying to god that the plane didn't go down. We shared the same DNA, after all.

Along with chipping in money to send me to two summers at Bennington College's Summer Program for high school students, where I studied poetry, fiction writing, and photography, Daddy Joe also got me out of the city for the occasional comic event. The one we were headed to was the biggest and farthest by far—the San Diego Comic-Con. He was scheduled to receive the Inkpot Award for a lifetime achievement in comics. My apartment was in the height of its chaos with my newborn sister, so I was grateful for the invite.

We landed in San Diego, and the next day, I stayed close to his side when we entered the awards ceremony. The hotel conference room was starkly white, with round tables scattered around the back of the room, and everyone facing a makeshift stage and podium. I watched him with silent pride as he shook people's hands, and I nodded and smiled as others told me what a legend he was. He wore a soft periwinkle button-up with a stiff white collar. His tie was dark blue with braided silver lines. It looked like it was meant for Hanukkah.

"Kirby and I actually got fired from Marvel," he told the crowd from the stage, smiling mischievously. "We had been negotiating with DC. DC didn't know what to do with us. We kind of hung around, working on new characters, but they also gave us some of their old characters to work on. We did a pretty terrible job on those. . . . We came up with Manhunter, which was kind of a theft of a motion picture at that time. A hunter that went after the Nazis. His greatest prey was man."

That first appearance of Manhunter, in the April 1942 issue of *Adventure Comics*, marked a milestone for Daddy Joe and Jack Kirby—their names on the cover, something that wasn't typically done at the time.

Their work on Sandman, a character that was already three months old before Daddy Joe and Jack inherited it, was first introduced in *Adventure Comics* #69, in December 1941. The costume was an obvious imitation of Batman's, and the hero came complete with a sidekick called Sandy the Golden Boy. The character was headed for the chopping block, but when Daddy Joe and Jack got their hands on Sandman, they gave him a second chance at life. Their creativity was powerful, exciting, and magical, and their art on *Adventure Comics* #84 broke the fourth wall, Sandman pointing out toward the reader and saying, "Nobody leave this magazine . . . A crime has been committed!!!"

While at DC, Daddy Joe and Jack were told to cut down on their hay, the term for their cross-hatching shading technique.

"No more hay, no more hay, they kept telling us," Daddy Joe said from the award stage. "And I said, 'Hey, we have a contract.'"

Most of the comics at DC were very slick in their style. Daddy Joe and Jack had their own style, and they did well with it. *Boy Commandos* was the bestselling book during their reign, selling more than Batman and Superman.

As I remember it, I met Stan Lee in that San Diego conference room for the first and only time. But it could have been back in 1993 or 1994, when Daddy Joe took me along to a comic convention in Philadelphia. For that convention, we were driven in a stretch limousine that had free bottles of water and cans of soda, and two phones on either side. I brought a disposable camera with me for the trip, and we snapped pictures of each other holding both phones to our ears, or holding a can of Pepsi in the air, grinning over the luxury of it all.

Daddy Joe met Stan Lee back in 1940 while serving as the first editor in chief of Timely Comics, which would later become Marvel. Daddy Joe's boss at Timely, Martin Goodman, asked him to hire his wife's seventeen-year-old nephew, Stanley Lieber. "Goodman just wanted me to give him some busy work," Daddy Joe explained. He started by having Stan sharpen pencils and get coffee; then, after some time, he gave him more creative assignments like story writing. After only a year or two, Daddy Joe and Jack Kirby, who were now working together at Timely, parted ways with Goodman over a financial dispute, and so a young Stan Lee took over as editor in chief at the age of nineteen.

Daddy Joe created his own Spider-Man in 1953. Just like the eventual Marvel character, Daddy Joe's Spiderman possessed insect-inspired superpowers—like walking up walls—though his came from a magic ring. His name changed a couple of times; first to "The Silver Spider," and then to "The Fly," the name under which Daddy Joe and Jack sold the character to Archie Comic Publications. But even after selling the Fly, the original Spiderman logo remained, sitting in piles of other ideas to be used at a later date.

When Martin Goodman announced that he was going to shut down Atlas, formerly Timely and soon to be Marvel, Stan asked Daddy Joe to meet him at Carnegie Deli. He was terrified of losing his job with Goodman and wanted to discuss his next moves.

"Start your own business," Daddy Joe told him.

But Stan didn't need to do that. Goodman ended up holding on for a bit longer. In Daddy Joe's book *The Comic Book Makers*, he writes, "[Stan] Lee called Kirby in and asked him if he had any comic characters lying around that hadn't been used. As I learned years later, Jack brought in the SPIDERMAN logo that I had loaned him before we changed the name to the Silver Spider." Stan handed the character over to Steve Ditko, who immediately recognized it as "Joe Simon's The Fly," and then took it in a different direction. Marvel was eventually saved with the success of Kirby and Stan's *Fantastic Four* in 1961, and a year later, Ditko's new and improved Spider-Man.

Over the years, I asked Daddy Joe what the deal was with Spider-Man and Stan Lee. "Wasn't it your idea?"

He waved his hand at me in a dismissive way. He didn't want to talk about it. But I saw the success that Stan Lee had, and I wanted that for Daddy Joe.

Wherever it was that I met Stan Lee, I was consumed with jealousy. Believing myself to be Daddy Joe's soldier, I gave Stan the cold shoulder that night at the convention. I nodded a curt hello, gave a stiff smile, and congratulated myself on not succumbing to his stardom as others in the room had.

A decade earlier, Daddy Joe called Stan and confronted him about the credit for Captain America going to him in newspapers and the media. "You know, I was really pissed off at you for all those stories I heard about you creating Captain America. It's all over the place!"

"Joe, I never said that. I even sent letters to the papers to tell them it isn't true. I was really pissed off about that. Jack was pissed off. You both have every right to be pissed off. I don't know what to do about it. I spell it out in all of the books I've published," Stan replied.

"I believe you," Daddy Joe said, and they ended the call cordially, with promises of a meetup next time Stan was in New York.

While I dwelled on what could have been, Daddy Joe was thrilled to see Stan. People watched with enthusiasm as Joe Simon and Stan Lee—two comic book legends—hugged, laughed, and reminisced about the old days.

The day after the San Diego awards ceremony, Aimee, a friend from Bennington, flew down from San Francisco to meet me. While the two of us hung out with some new punk friends, smoking cigarettes on the top level of the hotel parking lot, Daddy Joe stood in front of the building smoking his nightly cigar and making small talk with convention participants. Aimee and I later snuck into the hotel room, climbing silently into the queen bed next to his. The TV was still on, his snoring muffled under the blanket. He never questioned what we were doing all night in the parking lot. He just let me be.

FOURTEEN

A Failed Escape

1998

𝕏

We're going out to a movie, so you're going to babysit tonight," my parents told me. "We'll give you ten dollars."

I didn't want ten dollars. I wanted to get out of the apartment and get stoned with my friends. I wanted to drink from the forty-ounce bottle of fruity beer that was most likely being passed around in someone's apartment. I whined, I pleaded, but the plan was already set in stone. As my parents headed out the door, my brother in his pajamas looking up at me expectantly, my baby sister already in bed, I fought the urge to claw the walls like an animal.

In an attempt to get out of the apartment more, I took an after-school job at the East Side bread shop Ecce Panis. It was quaint, mimicking a country store, with only two people working at a time. Every night after a shift, I came home with a paper bag filled with the unsold breads of the day. There was the famous chocolate bread, and the toasted brioche that I spread almond butter over, toasted, and then sprinkled with confectioners' sugar.

Some evenings, I worked alongside a college-aged girl who made no effort to hide her displeasure of working with me. One night she decided that we should close the shop five minutes early, and I nodded, hoping to seem laid-back and cool. We locked the door and began our nightly routine of throwing what we could fit into one bag to bring home, and putting the rest in large garbage bags to be donated to a homeless shelter.

We rolled our eyes at each other when we heard the knock on the glass door. I continued to shovel chocolate bread into my own bag while my coworker unlocked the door and peeked her head out to apologize for the inconvenience of our closing. But this guy didn't care about the bread. From the corner of my eye I saw a black leather jacket push its way through the door.

"I have a gun," the man said.

His hand remained in his coat pocket. In hindsight, I assume he didn't actually have a gun, but in that moment, I figured it was a small yet powerful pistol.

Still new to the job and clueless to everything but the free bread, I stood at the register pushing buttons like a playful toddler, trying to get it to open.

He started to get impatient. "Hurry up!" he yelled, which just made me more nervous and led to continued bumbling at the register. My coworker pushed me out of the way like a fed-up mother, opened it in a flash, and let him grab what was in there—maybe $200.

"Turn around and count to one hundred."

We counted, pausing a few seconds after hearing the door close, then peeking over our shoulder and exhaling with a few *oh my god*s and an awkward hug.

After we called the police, I dialed home to let my parents know that I could have died but didn't. "We just got held up. The police are on their way."

I could hear my brother playing with his toy cars in the background, one of the cars screaming for help.

"Oh my god!" my mom exclaimed.

"I'll call you in a bit," I said, trying to sound strong.

"Okay. Let me know what the police say." Before the receiver went down, I heard her yelling to my dad across the apartment. "Papa! Megan just called, she got—" The phone went dead.

At the police station, we looked over hundreds of mug shots while being told, "We probably won't find him." Soon, the detective said I could call my parents and have them come get me; my coworker left with her dad without saying goodbye.

My dad sighed into the phone before asking "Can you just take a cab home?" I knew my parents were tied down with two young kids, but his disinterest in coming to my rescue only fueled my resentment.

The detective who'd shown me the mug shots offered to drive me home.

"You should keep an eye out while we drive," he said from the driver's seat of his Crown Victoria, as if the guy who robbed me would pop up at any second. I watched Madison Avenue, dark and empty, roll by and decided it was all a sham. That bread store with its cute little door and one quaint lock was bullshit.

FIFTEEN

No Room for the Rage

1998

"Okay, it's my turn," I said, holding out my hand toward the balloon that had just been filled with nitrous oxide.

I sat against a wall in someone's apartment, their parents gone for the weekend. An acquaintance, Carlos, was in charge of releasing the nitrous oxide from the whipped cream canister into the balloon, creating the whippet. Taking the balloon from his hand, I put the end of it in my mouth and inhaled deeply a few times until everything slowed down, the world almost coming to a standstill. Carlos began to move his hands in fluid swirls in front of my face, enjoying his own private rave. The sounds of helicopters beat against my eardrums.

It was just me, the thumping against my ears, and Carlos's hands moving. And then black.

I woke up with my head on the ground and my friend Hannah, her straight black hair long enough to tickle my cheeks, shaking my shoulder. "Are you okay?"

My head was pounding. "Why does my head hurt?" I asked, rubbing it.

"Holy shit, you were convulsing," she said, now sitting back on her heels.

I turned over to look at the rusted radiator next to my head. Some of the cobwebs from beneath it had collected in my hair. Even when unconscious, my body had been beating against the wall, unable to find room.

※

Back home things were getting worse.

"I fucking hate you!" I growled at my mom from behind the sliding glass wall that separated my bed from the living room.

We couldn't occupy the same space, physically or emotionally, without resentment and hostility coming to the surface. Our fights usually started with slight bickering, a small nag from my mom about leaving my homework on the dining room table or leaving the toes of my shoes sticking out in the walking path of our five-by-five foyer.

"What did you say to me?" she yelled from the doorway of the kitchen.

I jumped off my bed and marched my way to her, past the futon and up the one shallow step that separated the living room from dining room. I wanted to push her, hit her, to transfer this unbearable frustration and rage.

Instead, once I faced her, I moaned, "Just shut up!"

The words were barely out of my mouth before my face exploded with electricity—my cheek stinging, burning like the rest of my body in its rage. My dad had been the one who spanked me as a child; my mom never laid a hand on me. But the apartment, the storm we were creating, proved to be too much for the both of us.

I turned around, grabbed my bag, and walked out the door.

When I was seven years old, my mom dropped me off at a playdate and kissed me on the cheek so hard, sucking the flesh of my cheek with her lips, that my tooth came loose. Her affection for her children was often aggressive, as if she loved us so much, she could eat us whole.

Now that I was no longer a child, there wasn't aggressive love, just pure anger. I resented the feeling of being in the way, and she was fed up with my daily mood swings. I threw daggers at her with my words, words that no one should say to their mother. Together, with my teenaged hormones and her newborn exhaustion and postpartum hormones, we set the apartment ablaze.

My body still buzzed as the number 1 train carried me down to Fifty-Ninth Street. My anger bounced off the edges of my body and up the gray and cracked subway station stairs. It followed me out onto the street, ricocheting against the charged atoms of the city air. It sat between the fingers of my clenched fists, through the front door of Daddy Joe's building.

When I walked past the doorman, he looked up from his newspaper to nod hello, and I rode the elevator up to the sixth floor. I let my fingertips drag against the popcorn walls of his hallway—an attempt to leave the frustration there—all the way to the end, to apartment 6M.

But even with the residual angst that stubbornly stuck with me on my journey from uptown, my shoulders relaxed and my head cleared as I pushed open his heavy metal door. There was an instant relief as the bolt lock clanked loudly against the doorframe behind me and he swiveled around in his ratty leather chair with a smile.

"You know your mother loves you very much," Daddy Joe said an hour later.

I grunted a teenage acknowledgment from his drawing table, which held scraps of paper, ink stains, and my half-eaten Chinese takeout.

He watched me uneasily from his chair, uncomfortable with the sharp edges of my relationship with my mom. But he didn't push any further. He never did, and that was the beauty of our relationship. We didn't need to go any deeper than this. Like a long-married couple, we were comfortable sitting in silence. He watched his football game, and I dabbled with his colored pencils or raided the candy drawer at the bottom of his metal filing cabinet. We existed comfortably together, orbiting gracefully inside his small apartment, Captain America watching from the walls.

The truth was that I didn't want to bring the emotional burden of what was found in apartment 1K into Daddy Joe's place. I didn't want to tarnish my refuge with the anger that bounced off my mom and me, that furious ping-pong match. At home, I was a spinning top, unable to find a place to land safely. In his apartment, I was at peace.

He turned back to the TV, and I looked up from my plate of noodles. I studied his face, his eyes the same almond shape as my mom's, his arms and legs seeming to melt into the leather of the chair, tufts of soft white hair brushing against the headrest. I wondered if he was annoyed with my visits—if I was as much of a nuisance to him as I was to my parents. Had I overstayed my welcome? When he complained about his daughters—their life choices or the way they nagged him—I nodded with understanding, but really, I panicked that he thought the same about me. Did he think I was a bitch, too?

He coughed, a long, guttural, phlegm-clearing push, breaking me from my trance. "Was there any soda left in the fridge?" he asked.

"I don't think so."

He got up and headed toward his hallway closet that stored his bottles of soda, towels, and sheets. Sliding open the accordion-style door, he jumped back in surprise. "Oh, excuse me, ma'am!" he said, apologizing to an imaginary naked woman.

I shook my head. It was one of his favorite jokes. I knew he was ready to move on from the topic of my mom and me. I leaned back in his desk chair, swiveling right to left.

SIXTEEN

How We Cope

1998

Ж

Daddy Joe had two great loves: Harriet and art. With his comics, he had a hand in everything—the artwork, the writing, and the business. But with this overarching talent, he struggled to be seen as he wanted.

In an interview with the *Comics Journal*, Daddy Joe was asked about his role in the Simon and Kirby creations. "I think it's generally understood that you were more the business end of the partnership and Jack was more the creative end," the interviewer asked.

"That's bullshit. I mean, that's a myth," Daddy Joe responded with his typical candor. "In almost everything we did in those days I would sit down at the board and put everything in pencil, and Jack would . . . tighten it up. There came times when we would work different ways. . . . In those days, that's the way we did it."

From the time he was a little boy, he was an artist. In the third grade, he drew small cowboys and other tiny illustrations and sold them to classmates for a nickel. Creating on a blank canvas was what drove him, made the blood run through his veins. As a father, and then as a grandfather, he couldn't attend a child's birthday party without parking himself at a picnic bench and sketching one Casper the Friendly Ghost (not his creation, but a kid favorite) after another for hours. If he wasn't eating or filming with his video recorder, he was drawing.

For over thirty years, Daddy Joe supplemented his comic book work, which was typically hit or miss, with advertising gigs. The advertising business still let him use his artistic talent, as well as offering a stable source of income. One of the advertising supplements he did for the *New York Times* was a painting for the United States Olympic team, featuring Caitlyn Jenner, hands in the air, running through finish-line tape.

)(

But his heart was always with comics. In the early sixties, he took a meeting with the financier Teddy Epstein, a publisher for Crestwood Publications, who wanted Daddy Joe to start a magazine like *MAD*. Daddy Joe had his doubts about the project, but he agreed to the job, trusting Epstein's instinct that it was a trend worth pursuing.

To the delight of Epstein and Daddy Joe, the first issue of *Sick* did wonderfully. The magazine was a self-admitted rip-off of *MAD*, and Daddy Joe and the other artists on staff walked the line of lawsuit with each issue. They believed a lawsuit from Bill Gaines, the *MAD* publisher, would make for some great publicity. But Gaines was a friend of Daddy Joe's, and he laughed at his intentions. Gaines was doing very well for himself and would never waste money on a lawsuit.

A few years later, Epstein was having financial difficulties, and he paid Daddy Joe a visit at his house. He was sorry to say that he was selling *Sick* to Pyramid Books, and unfortunately, because the copyrights were registered to his company, Daddy Joe wouldn't get any money from the sale.

After Daddy Joe lamented to Harriet about the disappointing turn of events, she reminded him of the contract he had Epstein sign at the start of their partnership. The first sentence read: "You [meaning Epstein] have expressed a desire to publish my [meaning Daddy Joe's] title, *Sick* magazine."

Epstein's signature at the end of the contract sealed Daddy Joe's hold on the copyright. Epstein, after being scolded by his lawyer, tried to negotiate, but Harriet took the phone each time, demanding 75 percent of the sale. Finally, they settled on 50 percent. Daddy Joe figured Epstein would despise Harriet after the whole ordeal, but he sent her flowers after everything was finalized.

"Everyone loved Harriet," Daddy Joe told me more than once.

X

In 1969, Harriet was diagnosed with Hodgkin's disease. Two years later, my grandmother, only forty-eight years old, lost her battle with the disease. My mom was fourteen.

In the comic world, destruction and terror were easily fought off with a superhero. But there wasn't a superhero Daddy Joe could create to face the real-life tragedy of losing his wife.

Harriet's death left Daddy Joe with five teenage children, one of whom, a son, Jon, was autistic and schizophrenic and would often watch his sisters sleep from the dark doorways of their bedrooms.

"Where's Mom?" Jon asked for months after Harriet's death. He was about twenty years old, but confused and searching for his mother as if he were half that age.

Daddy Joe felt helpless, unconvinced that he could care for his son the way Harriet had. He found a group home nearby for Jon to live in that was staffed with nurses.

My mom brought me to meet him once when I was a toddler. "Did he understand who I was?" I asked years later.

"No," she said. "He didn't even understand who I was."

My mom stopped visiting him after that, and I learned to stop asking about him. He was part of a larger loss—a mother gone too soon, a family changed forever.

The family was without an anchor, and they all scattered within the next three years, going about their own lives, sometimes randomly orbiting in the same place at the same time. Daddy Joe escaped to the city soon after. The house, its memories, were too heavy to hold.

The heartbreak took the breath from him and his energy for his comics. He stopped working for a year, returning to the purist form of his first true love—a blank canvas and some paints. He had to put the business side of his creativity to rest for a while and explore his artistic depths. It was almost a primal response to grief. No expectations, just a release. Back to who he had been from day one.

One of his favorite pieces from that time is a painting of an old woman in a dimly lit hallway. It's dark and moody, nothing like his bright comics, and was hung on his apartment wall. He didn't talk about his heartbreak, but looking at that painting—the solemn old lady surrounded by shadows, the walls almost touching her shoulders—I could see the sorrow that he kept buried. I hated that he was forced to carry that ache. I hated that no one was able to save her, or save him.

X

Much like Daddy Joe, I found an escape in art. I scribbled poetry in notebooks as freely as the breath left my body. Most of the time, the words didn't seem to make sense. They were thoughts that I extracted, line by line, slowly from my throat. At high school parties, I would join my friends in the festivities, screeching and twirling, pretending to be the Spice Girls performing, our beepers clipped to the insides of our jean pockets. But soon, I'd find a corner to sit in with my pen and paper while they continued to play. The words fell from me, and I left my unbearably heavy feelings—frustrations with the boy I liked, feeling misunderstood by my parents—on the pages.

Watching Daddy Joe at his art table, day after day, year after year, showed me that art could be your everything. He was living proof that there could be success in doing something that you loved. Art ran rampant in my family, on both sides. Aunt Gail became a painter, Aunt Missy a jewelry designer, my paternal grandparents were both artists, and my dad's sister was also a jewelry designer.

Daddy Joe's parents used to read *True Confessions*—stories of love and romance—and there was one issue that sponsored a writing contest: "Tell us the story of how you and your husband met and fell in love." Daddy Joe remembered the two of them sitting at the table writing their story, focused and intent. His mother couldn't write very well, so she dictated the words to his father. That image of them putting this effort, this dedication, into a piece of writing stuck with him.

My dad was an artist, too, but it was hidden beneath his responsibilities of a husband and father. By day he was an estimator for construction projects, but at home, his creations brightened our childhoods. My dad turned my brother into a turtle one Halloween by weaving together pieces of cardboard and carefully painting the shell with green, black, and red detail—an exact replica of a turtle shell, with elastic bands to hold it against my brother's back. There were cardboard school buses painted bright yellow and cardboard towers. Even though we didn't have a backyard to play in, our living room held new surprises every now and then.

On the weekends, my dad took classes down at the Art Students League on West Fifty-Seventh Street, where he sketched voluptuous naked women and old sagging men with a thick piece of charcoal. Later, he taped them up on the living room bookshelf to show off his work, or maybe just to remind himself that art was still there for him.

λX

Soon, my poetry, my escapes with friends, and the warmth of Daddy Joe's apartment weren't quite enough. The fights with my parents got worse—my college escape, tantalizingly close, served as a catalyst for my intense yearning to break free. I became vicious with my words, hurling curses, slamming schoolbooks against the furniture, while my mom came at me like a lion tamer. She knew how to push my buttons, and I didn't know how to reset them.

As we fought, my baby sister crying, my six-year-old brother bouncing a ball against the wall, my dad becoming annoyed with all the fighting, and my mom and I ready to explode—it was our own urban tornado.

During one of these fights, at the beginning of my senior year, I locked myself in the bathroom—sitting on a damp rug, my back pressed against the bathroom door, my knees to my chest. I was angry at my parents for making us live in this small apartment, for treating me like an inconvenience, for continuing to yell from the other side of the door. The apartment wasn't big enough for our rage, and my usual escapes felt too far from shore to help.

There was no logical reasoning happening in my brain. For whatever reason—my hormones? my incessant need for solitude?—my body was on fire. I hated the apartment. I was untethered, unloved. I picked myself up off the bathroom floor and sat on the closed toilet seat. My face wet and red, I looked around the bathroom, searching for something to save me, to keep me afloat. I scanned the walls, the wicker basket holding washcloths and scrunchies, the mirrored medicine cabinet with floral inlay at the top.

I spotted a razor on the rim of the bathtub, almost hidden by the white shower curtain. It was exactly what I was looking for. I picked it up and studied it, the blade new, barely used.

Slowly, timidly, I dragged it across my forearm. I didn't want to die. I wanted everything to go somewhere else—like a spirit leaving a body. I was creating an emergency exit for whatever was boiling under my skin.

A red line appeared on my arm, and my frustration left my body in small puffs of release. But something replaced it—embarrassment over feeling sorry for myself, because self-pity was a quality my parents often criticized. I was an emotional, overly sensitive child, and the razor dragging against my arm, me sitting pathetically on the toilet seat, was just proof of this.

Even though the razor worked to offer a sense of immediate relief, my self-judgment kept me from doing it again. I was too self-conscious about being "that girl"—the girl I could imagine my parents rolling their eyes at.

I hid the cut marks under my sleeves when I came out of the bathroom, but a part of me wanted my mom to see them. I thought that maybe if she saw the extreme I had been forced to, she would be overwhelmed with sympathy. Maybe she would reconsider her opinions of my outbursts. Rather than assuming my aggravation stemmed from being a crazy teenager, she would understand that there was more to it. I was unhappy and feeling out of control of my situation— something that would always be difficult for me. I fantasized about her taking me into her arms and telling me that she understood my frustration, that all would be calm again. And so, the next day, I rolled up my sleeves.

"What are those marks?" she asked.

"Nothing," I said, already regretting my decision to let her see them, and rolled down my sleeves again. I was relieved that the secret was out, but she didn't ask anything more.

※

In my high school's lounge, my classmates Kurt and Remy started swatting me playfully with couch cushions until I lost my balance and landed on the couch. "Get off!" I screamed with laughter.

"Take that!" they yelled. I was thrilled with their attention. Their swatting slowed, and they took a moment to catch their breaths. I went to get up, thinking the game was over.

"I don't think so!" Kurt announced, and threw the pillow over the top half of my body, taking a seat on my head. "Get her legs," he ordered Remy. Soon my whole body was weighed down under them.

I continued to giggle with their attacks, but after a minute of squirming and kicking, I noticed the air beneath the pillow becoming hot and thick. I began to panic. I stopped, reasoning that if I stayed still and didn't engage, they would understand that I was done—a technique I used with my little brother all the time. I tried to focus on my breath, conserving whatever air was leaking through.

As a kid, I found comfort in small, dark spaces. Within the dark confines of my toy chest I created my own universe. Sometimes I'd stay in there until the air started to get thick and uncomfortable. But under the cushions, there was only panic building, the what-ifs mounting in my head: What happens if I run out of air? What if I pass out and they don't realize until it's too late? I was trapped. I was out of control. It was my nightmare.

Finally, they became bored with the game and jumped off. I immediately bolted upright, pushed past them, and ran straight for the school's front door, gasping and crying in the sunlight.

SEVENTEEN

The Great Escape

1999

)(

My college search was frantic. Desperate to be out of the apartment, I gobbled up whatever option was thrown my way.

I visited a friend at Hampshire College in western Massachusetts, where I interviewed for admission. That night, I stayed up until dawn drinking beers and smoking weed before curling up under a blanket on the floor of my friend's room. The taste of freedom made it hard to sleep.

My high school's history teacher served as the college guidance counselor, and after reviewing my grades, she circled ten schools that she considered sure bets. I wasn't a bad student, but without the help of SAT prep classes like the other kids were getting, my score wasn't a selling point for schools. From her list, I narrowed it down to the schools within driving distance, as a plane ride back and forth would be too expensive, and the application fees put a limit on my choices.

One weekend, my dad drove me to look at SUNY New Paltz, where my mom had gone, just under two hours from the city. We took advantage of the trip out of the city and went to the DMV to get my learner's permit—another ticket toward freedom, even though I wouldn't buy my first car until I was twenty-five.

100 . MEGAN MARGULIES

I eventually decided on Wheaton College in Massachusetts, and soon after, I found myself sitting across from Daddy Joe, hoping he could help with my biggest escape yet. He was in his brown leather chair, and I sat at his drawing table with pen in hand, nervously doodling on a scrap of drawing paper. I asked him to cosign a student loan so that I could go to college.

"So how much do you need?" he exhaled. Everyone in the family came to him when they needed financial help, and I could tell it wore on him.

"Nothing. I don't need any money, just for you to cosign the private student loans."

I pressed the pen down harder on the paper, the line growing darker, the ink starting to spread outward.

"Why can't your parents cosign?"

"The bank won't accept them as cosigners. They already took out a federal loan."

He stayed silent, keeping his eye on the city view outside his window. The clock on his wall ticked.

"Whatever you need," he said, unmuting the TV and bringing the apartment back to life.

"Thank you. I promise I'll keep up with the payments."

An instant replay of a football player being tackled moved in slow motion across the screen. "Whatever you need, baby," he said again.

Nine months later, I said goodbye to New York. As we drove north, the city receding in the rearview mirror, I thought of Daddy Joe in his midtown apartment. I was removing myself, cutting a few of the tightly wound ropes that held me to the city. I knew that he would always be my beacon of light in a city that would never be mine again.

X

My dorm room was on the first floor of a concrete building in Norton, Massachusetts, a small working-class town forty minutes south of Boston. The building looked like a prison, but it was a beautiful sight to me. The campus represented the next chapter of my life—*freedom*.

There was a bunk bed and a single bed crammed into my room, the co-ed bathrooms down at the end of the cinder-block hall. I threw my backpack onto the bottom bunk, claiming it, before my roommates arrived.

"Do you need another blanket?" my mom asked, always ready to throw another quilt on a problem.

I shrugged. "I don't think so."

My dad worked on bringing my stuff in from the car while my sister waddled up and down the hallway. My brother leaned his head against the metal doorframe of the room, watching my mom and me inspect the closet space and the windows to see how far they slanted open.

"It's important to air out rooms every day," she said. I was on my own now; I needed to remember these things.

With my belongings piled in the corner of the room, and nothing left to inspect, my parents said that they needed to hit the road. We looked at one another, wondering how to do this—how to say goodbye and release me into the wild.

My dad hugged me. "Love you." He smelled the top of my head as he did in meaningful moments, breathing in, and exhaling a "My girl."

My mom and I hugged awkwardly. "Call me later," she said with a sniff. Her lips began to purse. She was trying not to cry.

"Stop!" I laughed, feeling tears threatening to form. I knew the apartment would be calmer without me there, rid of the constant buzz of frustration. Wasn't she excited to get me out? As excited as I was to get out?

But that's the thing about change, even if it's necessary. It's scary. Exciting and terrifying. I didn't realize that this moment could be sad for her. Who would I be with this newfound freedom? Who would my mom be without her angsty teenager hiding in the shadows?

When my family left, I began marking my territory. I figured I was better prepared for the dorm life than most of the other kids here. It was a tiny room for three people, but the wall next to my bed was mine. I taped up close to twenty photographs of high school friends. I could put whatever I wanted on these walls, express myself however I wanted. It was both thrilling and unnerving.

The most important decoration was the small square of white cloth upon which a friend had painted the Captain America shield. I placed it in the middle of my photograph collage. I still had the comfort of Daddy Joe to wake up to every morning in this new life. He was a constant presence, one part of my previous life that I was unwilling, unable, to shed.

)X(

I was different than the other girls at school. Most of them were products of traditional homes. They had duvets that matched their sheets and pillowcases, dust ruffles, and photos in flowery frames. But I found comfort in my mismatched sheets and blankets. The sheets and pillowcases were a worn green or blue that were soft and familiar. A brown, blue, and yellow quilt stitched merely for the necessity of warmth was folded at the foot of my bed. I enviously eyed their Apple laptops, with their bright colors and little handles on the top. Luckily, I was loaned an old PC from the school's computer department so I could type assignments and log into AIM. Daddy Joe quickly learned how to use instant messenger, and we chatted a few times a week.

I gravitated toward a small group of city kids because they felt like home, even if it was a home that I'd been eager to escape. They were an anchor in a strange land of blondes driving Range Rovers and BMWs.

During our first week of school, as I smoked a cigarette on the front step of my dorm, I overheard someone talking about New York. Their friend pointed to me. "Megan's from New York, too."

"What part of New York?" the girl asked, seemingly unimpressed, her teeth perfectly straight and perfectly white, her hair like corn silk.

"The city," I said.

"Yeah," she said, annoyed, "but *what* part?" There was obviously a "dumbass" left off the end of her sentence.

"West Ninety-Sixth Street," I said.

My eagerness to make a new friend completely vanished. I was ready to walk away, to leave it at that, but I had to prove something to myself. There was no way this girl had grown up in a tiny rent-controlled apartment. No way she had drooled over houses with multiple bedrooms and bathrooms. I bet she'd even had her own bathroom, to go along with her own bedroom. I decided that her daddy had also bought her an expensive car before sending her off to college loan-free.

"What about you?" I asked.

"Riverdale," she said, bored with me.

I nodded, pleased with the accuracy of my prejudice. Riverdale, a wealthy enclave in the Bronx, felt like a faraway place. I didn't know much about it except for the mansions and manicured lawns. Later that year I published a poem about her called "Mimicking Manhattan" in the school's literary journal, the teenage, artistic version of a "fuck you."

X

It took some time to acclimate to my new surroundings. I loved my freedom, but I still had to learn to be comfortable with it.

I discovered my new city when I started dating Jake, a fellow freshman, who grew up in Boston's North End. On weekends, we stayed at his mom's apartment on Boston Harbor. Neither of us had a car, so we took the bus that ran from the school parking lot to the front of the Park Plaza Hotel in Back Bay.

At his mom's apartment, you could smell the salt water, almost feel the vastness of the ocean from the breeze that came through the screen. We spent nights sitting on the edge of the pier, passing a bowl back and forth, our legs swinging above the waves crashing against the gray stone below us. We could only see the lights of the airplanes coming and going from Logan Airport, the boats rocking, and the skyline of the city to our right.

During one of these trips, Jake and I sat on his bed after a night of wandering the neighborhood. His mom was already asleep in the next room. In the silence, Jake held his face in his hands and began to cry.

"What?" I asked, panicked that he was going to tell me he had cheated on me.

"I love you," he told me. "I'm sorry, it's crazy."

His words terrified and thrilled me. We had been dating for only two months, and even though I wasn't sure if what I was feeling was love, I told him I loved him, too.

We were inseparable. It was such a relief to feel that kind of love after years in my family's apartment, being nothing but a raging nuisance. I was *wanted*. Someone loved me urgently, in a way that was verbalized constantly. He began to feel like an integral part of me— like a limb—and although it took me a little bit longer, I learned that I loved him, too.

Jake gave me a new home. Boston felt different, maybe because I had my freedom there. But it was also a city lite. Boston had the familiar noise and energy, but it was calmer, cleaner. It reminded me of a movie set city. I was relaxed, not searching for an escape. Boston was a blank slate that could house my new, happier memories. My distance from New York and my old life became easier day by day.

EIGHTEEN

Midtown

2000

Ж

When I returned to New York for a visit, it was never for more than a few nights. I slept on a futon mattress on the floor next to my brother's and sister's beds. It was folded and pushed under my brother's bed during the day, and then pulled out before my siblings went to sleep, waiting for me to tiptoe to bed around midnight.

After being away, the city felt even more overwhelming. It carried the weight of all my past anxieties—the fear of walking home alone at night, the stress of being a teenager in the small apartment. Daddy Joe's apartment and hospitality became even more necessary. No visit to the city was made without a day with him—my chance to breathe and feel as though I was welcome, belonged.

"I'll be there tomorrow around noon," I told him when I arrived for spring break. He wouldn't be up for the day until then. "Email me a list of what you want from the store." He loved his computer, a slow Dell that was infuriating to use and crashed constantly.

"Sounds good, baby."

His email came in an hour later: *Yo... baby...If you are convenient with the place that sells those chocolate crepes please pick up some more. If not, next time.... Lentil beans....bacon....liverwurst......small tomatoes 5 bananas.....juice eggscinnamon buns.*

He was already awake when I arrived, a shopping bag in one hand, my purse on the opposite shoulder. The apartment smelled like coffee and chicken broth.

He swiveled around in his chair, a steaming mug of coffee in his hands. "I don't have pants on, don't be scared."

His skinny legs were translucent against the royal blue of his Captain America boxer shorts. I noticed his toenails, yellowed and too long. *If you were a good person, you would cut those for him*, I thought to myself. Instead, I kissed him on the cheek and put the groceries in the fridge.

"I got you that turkey and Brie sandwich you like," I called over my shoulder. "And some strawberries."

"Okay," he said, nodding. I threw my purse on the red futon and sat down across from him. He studied me for a moment. "You look beautiful."

I smiled. "Thanks."

"How long are you here for?"

"Leaving tomorrow."

He thought for a moment. "How's school?"

"Good. I got a poem accepted in the literary journal."

"I never went to college."

I nodded. He loved to tell me this.

"And look how stupid I am!" He laughed, his coffee-less hand in the air. "Want to see what I'm working on?"

He rocked, once, twice, and heaved his body off his chair, moving only a few feet away to the black chair at his art table. He placed his coffee on top of the pale wood taboret that had followed him for years. I learned the word "taboret"—a low table—from his story about being deposed during his 1999 Marvel lawsuit to retain the rights to Captain America.

"The guy kept pointing to a drawing of the office, labeled with names to show who was working during the time, and he kept saying,

'Who is this?' I'd ask who. He was pointing at the table. The guy was getting aggravated, saying, 'Him! Taboret!'"

In 1964, Marvel brought back Captain America for *The Avengers*, and a year later they did the same in a book called *Tales of Suspense*, credited to Stan Lee and Jack Kirby. Three of the stories in *Tales of Suspense* were created by Daddy Joe and Jack in 1940, before Stan Lee even arrived at Timely.

When the copyright for the first ten issues of *Captain America Comics* came up for renewal, Daddy Joe pounced. On the advice of his lawyers, he ended up settling for a disappointing amount. But in 1999, he was ready to fight again. A law passed in 1976 stated that authors could reclaim copyrights fifty-six years after the original registration. Daddy Joe filled out the paperwork again, Marvel filed suit, and Daddy Joe filed a countersuit. After five years and many annoying depositions—including the one with Mr. Taboret—they settled.

The best part of the settlement was the credit on every Captain America comic: "Created by Joe Simon and Jack Kirby."

Daddy Joe was finishing the lettering of an *Intimate Confessions* cover the day of my visit. "You conceited oaf!" a woman cried as she slapped a man across the face, his back to the reader and a startled red "Ow!" above his head.

"Women are crazy," Daddy Joe explained, as he darkened the "*f*" in "oaf."

I rolled my eyes and picked up a stacked pile of empty yogurt cups. He stopped and looked at my hands.

"That's not trash, you know. Don't let your mom get ahold of those. I use those to mix colors. So smart, right?" He went back to drawing the marital spat. "And this?" He pointed to the taboret and a spinning yellow contraption on top like a three-tiered wedding cake holding his brushes and X-Acto knives. "This was being sold for kitchen appliances. My brain works in mysterious ways, doesn't it?"

It was his mysterious brain, its constant tendency toward wonderment, that helped him come up with winning comic book ideas. In the late 1940s, Daddy Joe and Jack were looking for the next big thing. Daddy Joe remembered his parents reading true love stories back when he was a child, and he had long wondered why adults were reading comic books meant for children. It was time they created something for older girls, he thought, young women who were also in need of an escape from reality. The only comic books marketed for girls were *Archie* and *Punch and Judy*, and they didn't feel sufficient.

Daddy Joe did a quick mock-up of the first cover of *Young Romance*, with the blurb "Designed for the More Adult Readers of Comics." As Daddy Joe told it, after he finished the cover, he tucked it under his arm and crossed the street to Jack's house.

Roz, Jack's wife, was in the kitchen and nodded upstairs. "He's in the bathroom. He's been in there for days."

Daddy Joe said he would wait, but Roz assured him it wasn't digestive issues. Jack was busy painting the walls of the bathroom—a large mural of blue waters and tropical fish. After climbing the pull-down ladder to the attic, Jack and Daddy Joe settled into the studio, and Daddy Joe fell back on the couch. He showed him the cover. Jack loved it.

"It's time we go into business for ourselves!" Daddy Joe declared. But Jack reined him in, reminding him of the volatile nature of the comic book business. They decided to draw up an entire issue before showing it to a publisher. That way, they would have a head start if anyone tried to steal their idea. They eventually made the sale to Crestwood Publications.

Months later, on his way to the hospital where Harriet had just given birth to their first child, Daddy Joe saw a gaggle of girls around a newsstand. Peering over their shoulders, Daddy Joe saw, to his delight, that they were reading the first issue of *Young Romance*.

"Kirby and I knew it was a hit then," Daddy Joe recalled.

Young Love was released soon after and sold almost as well as *Young Romance*. Between the two titles, they sold almost two million copies per issue.

Daddy Joe wrote much of the love advice under the guise of Nancy Hale, and according to his eldest daughter, Missy, it taught her to be a "good girl" as she grew up. The twins, my mom and Aunt Gail, on the other hand, had to be watched. Every time one of them got dropped off by a boyfriend, Daddy Joe flipped on the floodlights in the driveway, released the Great Danes, and headed outside with a flashlight.

"Father!" a twin would yell, one foot still in the car, their curls glowing between the door and roof from the floodlights. "Get the dogs out of here!" The Great Danes danced frantically around the car, biting the air with each threatening bark.

"Hi. How's it going?" Daddy Joe asked, shining his flashlight in the wide eyes of the latest boyfriend, who usually sat frozen, clutching the steering wheel. With a slam of the passenger-side door and a wave, the poor guy was released and permitted to drive away to safety.

X

"I heard you have a boyfriend now?" Daddy Joe asked me, not taking his eyes off his *Intimate Confessions* cover, now with bright green paint in the title.

"I guess."

He looked at me. "You guess? Does Joe need to talk to him?"

"We just started dating," I said shyly, leaving out the confusing math of how many months we were just fooling around, plus the time it took to start falling in love.

"Are you getting married?"

"Oh my god, stop."

"Is he Jewish?"

"Adopted, but raised by a Jewish family."

"Uh-huh," he said, and nodded. He was phobic of religion after growing up in a conservative household. "You know, I'd like to live with the goys and be buried with the Yids."

Daddy Joe sat back in his chair, putting down his paintbrush. "In fact, I've been thinking about it, and I think I'm ready to go," he said.

I forced a smile. A heaviness settled in my stomach, and I looked away from him, pretending to study the artwork on the walls. He was an old man, but the thought of him dying and needing to be buried seemed impossible. He was our family's sun and our moon—he was our universe. Things that important didn't just disappear.

"Can you do a Captain America sketch I can bring back for Jake?" I asked, steering him away from his conversational detour.

"Sure!" he exclaimed, taking the bait. "Should I write something on it?"

"Yeah," I said, my stomach lightening again.

"*Yes*," he corrected me, reaching for a clean sheet of paper.

NINETEEN
Crumbling Down
2001

X

In an old home video of Daddy Joe, he walks into view of the camera wearing a black suit and maroon tie.

"Good evening, ladies and gentlemen. It's now February 14. And tomorrow I will die."

He takes a dramatic pause and then claps his hands together.

"It's okay. I'm ready. I'm going into surgery to repair this tooth here—that's not even injured! It's perfectly fine!" He grins at the camera, which is propped against an old printer on a shelf in his living room. It's hooked up to the television monitor so that he can see what the camera sees, a helpful feature, as he is alone in the apartment.

"When I'm gone," he continues, "it's a potluck. Come in and take whatever you want." He goes on to list everyone in the family—watching it years later, after I converted the videos to DVDs, I listened to him run down the list of family members, my heart sinking each time my name wasn't mentioned. But then he ends with, "And of course, Megan," and my heart swells again with vindication.

"You can throw these films away and never admit that I'm your grandfather," he tells his future audience. "Anyway, this is a living will." He unbuttons his suit jacket, shakes each side with vigor, imitating David Letterman, and walks out of frame to take off the suit. He hated wearing suits.

※

A few months before two airplanes flew into the towers of the World Trade Center, Daddy Joe almost came crumbling down.

When my mom arrived for one of her routine visits, she started the coffeemaker and then opened his bedroom door when she heard the squeaking of the bedsprings.

"Morning, Father," she said, sitting beside him on the edge of the bed. He didn't say a word. She assumed he was still groggy and coming out of his dream. "I made you coffee," she said, offering him the mug.

He brought it to his lips, but instead of swallowing, the coffee ran down his chin, dribbling on his thin cotton boxer shorts. He looked at her and tried to say something, but the words seemed to get stuck behind his wet lips. She called 911 and then wiped his face with a towel.

"He was so out of it," my mom whimpered over the phone to me when she called to tell me about his stroke. I was sitting in my dorm room, finishing up my sophomore year of college.

"But he's going to fine, right?" I asked. This was my typical response to any ailment to befall him. He had to be fine.

Despite everyone's concern, Daddy Joe insisted on returning to his apartment and living alone. But his heart medication dosage wasn't quite right, and he began to faint a lot. My mom found bruises along his hips from where he had landed the night before her visit.

"I'm fine, Lori," he insisted. "Look!" He pretended to speed-walk from the drawing table to the kitchen. But his left leg lagged behind.

"You can't live alone. Missy wants you to live with her for a while."

My mom's older sister was on Long Island, a little over an hour away, in Selden. Daddy Joe opposed the idea but knew he wasn't going to win this argument. His children were all in agreement.

He was phobic of losing his independence, of living in an elderly home, of using a wheelchair, even when his left leg continued to lag behind. On the day my parents arrived at his apartment to move him to Long Island, he refused the wheelchair again.

"How are we supposed to get you down to the car?" my mom asked him, irritated with his stubbornness. "What do you think, I'm going to carry you over my shoulder?"

"Oh, fuck you, Lori, I can walk just fine." He began to drag his leg to the front door, holding the wall for stability. "Do you have my paints? Pencils?"

"Father! You're going to fall. Here." She rolled his drawing table chair over to him. "Sit in this."

He eyed it, gave it a thought, and then accepted the offer. My dad held Daddy Joe's forearm and helped to ease him down into the chair. My mom held open the apartment door, and my dad pushed him out. When they emerged in the lobby, Daddy Joe waved to the doorman.

"I'm like the pope!" he exclaimed.

)(

My parents visited Daddy Joe out on Long Island every other weekend.

"When can I go home?" he asked during one of their visits.

"Soon, Father."

"Just put me in the car now. Break me out of this joint."

"You're not ready," my mom told him, handing him a napkin to wipe the soup off his chin. "You're living the life here. Missy is the best cook, right?"

He nodded.

When my parents said goodbye that afternoon and walked out to the car, Daddy Joe watched them from the open doorway.

"Bye, Father!" my mom called. "Behave yourself."

Watching their car pull away like a sulking puppy, he raised his middle finger in the air.

Ж

At the end of the summer, my mom and dad drove Daddy Joe back to the city. He was home, safe and sound, just in time to watch the sky turn purple that September, the collapsed towers smoldering and sending a stench all the way to midtown and his sixth-floor windows.

I was in my first days of junior year, taking a course on media. At the beginning of the Tuesday morning class, our teacher rolled out a television set.

"A plane hit the World Trade Center this morning," she told us.

"Idiot," I said to my friend Raul, who was also from New York. We assumed it was a Cessna plane, an inexperienced pilot trying to get a close-up view of the city and failing miserably.

We gathered around the small television set, some of us sitting on the floor. It came to life, glowing in the dim light of the classroom, showing the burning tower.

"It would be hard to believe that a small plane could cause that kind of damage," the news anchor said. They continued: *"Not a lot of wind, clear day, pilots of the commercial jets know to stay clear of these buildings. If this was an accident it would be a needle-in-a-haystack kind of accident.*

"Oh my god, another plane just went into the other tower."

I stood up, and left the room, my classmates, the television, those last words. I tried to catch my breath outside, tried to shake the sense of dread. New York was under attack. My home, my family. I began to picture more planes plummeting from the sky, landing all over the city, on top of the Upper West Side.

I pulled out my flip phone and dialed my parents' number. Busy signal. I hung up and dialed again. Busy signal. I hung up and dialed Daddy Joe's number. Busy. Raul came out of the building and sat next to me wordlessly.

"I can't get a hold of anybody," I told him. "All the lines are busy."

"I can't, either," he said.

I dialed my parents again. Busy.

I had spent years waiting for the day that I could escape the city, and now I wished I was there. I was helpless, useless, sitting on the grass in Norton. I wanted to give the city the respect of experiencing this horror, something that would forever change it, with all my friends and family still there. It wasn't fair that I didn't have to feel the rumbles, hear the explosions, watch the smoke billow toward the sky.

I found Jake outside our dorm building. I let my head rest against his chest.

"I can't believe both towers collapsed," he said.

I hadn't heard that news yet, and stayed in his arms while picturing the empty place in the skyline, a hole as heavy as the collapsed rubble. My parents' apartment, my dad's job, and my brother's school were all far enough uptown that I believed they were safe. But Daddy Joe was in midtown, his windows facing downtown. I worried about the wind changing direction and the smoke invading his apartment. He probably woke up close to noon, wondering what that smell was, turning on the TV to find what had happened right outside his window.

When the phonelines came back to life, my mom told me that the smell in the city was unbearable. Daddy Joe said that he had to keep his windows closed because he was sure that he smelled burning flesh.

I was surprised by my instinct to run home. New York was like an older sibling who had tested me for years. When someone asked me if I would ever move back, I usually shot back, "Hell no," with the same disdain I'd answer if they'd asked if I would like to drink from their toilet. But New York made things complicated. The city was fissured to me like the mantle to the core of the earth, whether I liked it or not.

That weekend, my school rented a bus to take all the New Yorkers home for the weekend. Because the city was shut down, not allowing any traffic in or out, we were dropped at Pelham Bay Park in the Bronx. From there, we boarded the 6 train south.

We were aboveground when we approached the East Side of the Manhattan skyline. Although it was early afternoon, the sky was purple, heavy as ink.

"Holy shit," someone said over the sounds of the tracks beneath us. We approached home but didn't recognize it. It was like walking into your house to find it smashed and burned, unrecognizable.

X

"Can you believe this?" Daddy Joe asked.

We spoke on the phone while I was in the city because he didn't like the idea of any of us coming farther downtown, where the air quality was worse.

"I haven't left my apartment yet," he added.

Instead, he got to work re-creating the first *Captain America* cover, but instead of Hitler being punched, it was Osama bin Laden getting a right hook. The art is dated September 11, 2001, with members of the Taliban standing behind bin Laden, firing away, as Bucky salutes from the bottom-right corner, wearing an FDNY baseball cap.

"I don't think you should show this to anyone," my mom said of the cover. "I don't want you getting beheaded."

Although it wasn't published, the cover was created with the same intention as the original. It represented what a lot of Americans fantasized about doing, the ones who were angry and hurt, who felt helpless. As an artist, Daddy Joe believed this was his way to become involved, maybe offer a perceived solace, even if it wasn't real.

I met Ro for a walk on Saturday afternoon. We headed down Broadway, our typical route to the Monument. Usually we powered down the street in our natural speed-walking state—we were true New Yorkers, after all. But on that day, we moved slowly. The whole city seemed to move in slow motion with us, muted. Strangest of all, everyone we passed or made eye contact with smiled warmly, tiredly. New York was in this together, and it was beautiful and heart-breaking.

I was in the city for only the weekend. The trip was planned for us to touch base with our loved ones, give them a hug, and reconnect with a home forever changed. My dad drove me back up to Pelham Bay that Sunday, and I boarded the bus again. My classmates and I were silent as we headed north, our weekends—the sounds, the heavy air—riding with us. The further away we got from the city, the clearer the sky became, the heavier my guilt for leaving.

The tragedy was a reminder that New York—even with all my anxieties about it—was my home, and always would be. It was where my loved ones lived, especially Daddy Joe with his finicky heart, tripping like a faulty wire. The city had left me a lifetime of baggage to lug around, but it was where my roots had first crept through the earth.

TWENTY

What We Hold On To

2004

Ӿ

I began to wonder if Jake was the man I was supposed to marry. I loved him deeply, but I wasn't sure if it was the kind of love that could survive a lifetime. I voiced my concerns to him for months, wondering out loud if the fact that I had never dated anyone else would be our ruin. He protested, insulted that I'd even consider ending our long relationship. I swayed between moments of conviction—moving on would be the best thing for both of us—and then disgust with myself for even considering letting go of something so good, so comfortable.

Even though it was hard to imagine my life without him—we had been dating for almost six years—I had a nagging feeling in the pit of my stomach. It was as if there was a piece missing in our gears. The tiniest screw that could go unnoticed for years, and one day just make everything fall apart.

Ӿ

After Harriet died, Daddy Joe dated here and there, but no one stuck. How could anyone replace that adorable creature who lay out in her bikini for hours on end? The ferocious cleaner who hated to cook?

"You should have seen all the women in the neighborhood who came knocking on our door only weeks after my mother died," my mom told me. "Disgusting."

His friend Carmine Infantino, who became publisher at DC the year that Harriet died, often brought a girlfriend with him during visits to Daddy Joe. Sometimes Carmine brought a friend for Daddy Joe, but he wasn't interested. But one day, Daddy Joe brought a woman along on a family outing. It was the first time he'd had someone new around the kids. My mom and Gail, both about fifteen years old, sat in the back seat of the car, unsure of what to make of this stranger. As Daddy Joe pulled out of their circular gravel driveway, the woman draped her arm around his neck. From the back seat, my mom watched this new arm resting on her father's neck—an intimate gesture that had once been reserved for her mother. She told me how the moment stuck with her, a knife in her heart—a confirmation that it would never again be her mother's arm around his neck.

Daddy Joe broke up with the woman soon after. None of his relationships lasted more than a month or two. But four years after Harriet's death, he met Rosie. There weren't fireworks, or a meet-cute, as he'd had with Harriet. But he genuinely liked her and enjoyed the company.

Rosie volunteered to drive Daddy Joe, my mom, and Gail on college tours in her large Cadillac. As they passed the historic buildings on campuses across the northeast, Frank Sinatra blasted from the impressive sound system. The twins slouched in the back seat, trying to hide their faces. It was the early 1970s, and they would have preferred the Beatles.

Rosie had a house in Jamaica, somewhere outside of Negril. The family went for a month in the winters, where the twins sampled Jamaica's finest marijuana and Daddy Joe enjoyed the reggae music coming from the small shacks along the beach. Rosie's house was next door to a Playboy villa, where the bunnies enjoyed the outside shower only partially hidden in a coconut grove.

LEFT: *Adventure Comics #84* (DC Comics, 1943) by Joe Simon and Jack Kirby. The issue that literally tested the boundaries of comic books by breaking the fourth wall.

BELOW: *Boy Commandos #2* (DC Comics, 1943). Cover pencils by Jack Kirby, inks by Joe Simon. During the Simon and Kirby reign, the Boy Commandos outsold Batman and Superman comic books.

RIGHT: *Boys Ranch* #6
(Harvey Comics, 1951).
The last issue in a six-issue
series about three young
boys—Dandy, Wabash, and
Angel—who operate a ranch
that was bequeathed to them.

BELOW: *Captain America* #2
(Timely Comics, April 1941).
Penciled by Joe Simon.

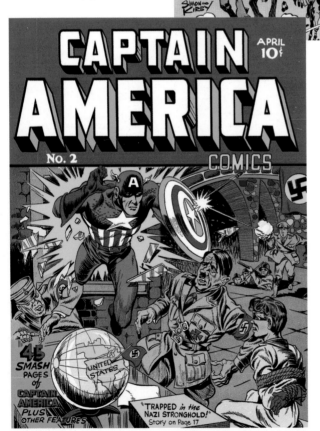

LEFT: *Captain America Comics* #1 (Timely Comics, March 1941). Cover art by Jack Kirby. Pencilers: Joe Simon and Jack Kirby.

BELOW: *Fighting American* #4 (Prize Comics, 1954). Penciled by Jack Kirby, Inked by Joe Simon. Features Rhode Island Red and her minions. The Fighting American series, fighting Cold War battles, lasted seven issues.

The Last Supper, by Joe Simon and Gail Simon. Upon hearing that Captain America might be killed off, Daddy Joe recreated Leonardo Da Vinci's famous painting of Jesus' Last Supper with his daughter, Gail.

Captain America is surrounded by other popular characters including The Red Skull, Captain Marvel, Spider-Man, and The Fighting American.

LEFT: Green Hornet #9 (Harvey Comics, 1942). Penciled by Jack Kirby and Inked by Joe Simon.

BELOW: Young Romance #3 (Prize Comics, 1948).

LEFT: One of my many visits home. We're standing next to his art table, one of Harriet's oil lanterns sits on top of his white storage shelf.

BELOW: Daddy Joe and me at a food festival that ran down Ninth Avenue. I picked out the beer can for him.

LEFT: Daddy Joe painting me like one of his creations. Behind us is the self portrait of him (with a nose job) and some of his most famous characters, and a painting that pays homage to the events in *Adventures of the Fly* #1

ABOVE: Taken by a professional photographer at his apartment. The photoshoot was for a book, but we snuck in a few personal shots. The original Captain America sketch that Daddy Joe gave to Martin Goodman is on the wall behind us.

"He would peer through the fence half the day," my mom told me.

But mostly Daddy Joe hung out with his kids. They enjoyed horseback riding through the hills, and he tried to show off the equestrian skills he had learned in the Coast Guard. Once, in an attempt to impress, he tried to jump onto his horse in one quick, fluid motion. He went right over, landing on the other side of the horse, laughing from the ground below, the horse shaking a fly off its nose.

Rosie hoped for more time with Daddy Joe. "What about me?" she asked him.

Though he loved her, he wasn't in love with her. There was a difference between caring for someone and feeling as if your two souls were fused, as he had with Harriet. He and Rosie broke up after a few years of dating. It had been his longest relationship since Harriet, but he discovered he would rather be alone.

X

The stories about Daddy Joe and how he'd never truly loved again after Harriet's death pushed me to take the plunge with my own love life. On October 12, 2004, the day after Daddy Joe's birthday, I asked to meet Jake around the corner from my job. I was an executive assistant for an art-funding nonprofit across the street from the Boston State House. He was working at a law firm in the Financial District, not far from me.

I cried before I could get the words out.

"What?" Jake asked defensively. He knew what was happening.

"I'm so sorry," I sobbed, wanting him to hold me.

He turned from me, facing the stone wall of the building, tourists and financial types weaving around us. He turned back to me, trying to fight back tears. "If this is what you want," he said, and walked away.

There's no such thing as a clean break. I continued to call him, to see him in group settings, and, of course, to sleep with him. It was unfair

of me, but erasing someone that important from my life was too difficult. A few months into our back-and-forth, he began to pull away.
He seemed cold when we saw each other, obviously trying to sever
whatever was still clinging between us. That February, he ended it for
good for the both of us.

That spring, we still both lived in the North End of Boston, and I
spotted him with a girl as I walked home from a coffee shop. We were
only twenty feet from each other, too late for me to turn around and
avoid being seen. They stopped as I approached, putting down their
Trader Joe's shopping bags, and Jake waved a hello.

"Hey," he said.

I kept my eyes down, too traumatized to look at them together, to
see him paired up with a new human, doing something as intimate as
food shopping together. I kept walking, right by them, down my block,
up the stairs, into my apartment, and facedown onto my bed.

I was officially untethered.

The end of the relationship ruined me. I lost fifteen pounds and
developed a rash on the side of my face from the heartbreak. My mom
spent countless hours on the phone with me, peppering me with words
of support, trying to help me find my anger and strength.

"The fact that he found someone new so quickly says something,"
she said.

"How could it be so easy for him?" I cried, itching the side of my
face. "Did he ever really love me?"

"Why don't you come home for a few days?"

The first night of my visit home, my mom pulled out her jewelry
box from the front hall closet and said she was looking for something to heal me. These weren't fancy or expensive jewels; they were
bracelets made from colorful beads, Native American earrings with
silver feathers hanging off the ends, a necklace that had a gold Star
of David embedded in a turquoise circle that Aunt Gail had gifted my
mom when they were in their late twenties. Among these pieces was a

ring that Harriet had given to my mom right before she died. It had a thin gold band and a small amethyst stone, and it fit perfectly on my ring finger. I often tried it on, twirling the band, thinking about how I was touching something that Harriet once held. Sometimes I believed Harriet's energy radiated from the band.

I came over and put Harriet's ring on my finger as I always did, studying the small stone.

"Do you want it?" my mom asked, using her pinky to sort through her small treasures. "I can pass it down to you. It'll be like she's watching over you."

I was stunned. I could only keep the ring on my finger and mutter a small "Yeah."

Later, in Daddy Joe's apartment, I showed him the ring. "It fits me perfectly," I said. I could tell that it pained him to see it, so I put my hand down and out of his view.

He shuffled to the kitchen. "You're going to be okay, Megan," he said.

TWENTY-ONE

Loving and Losing, A Reminder

2007

М

y heartbreak was a reminder of another threat of loss. I knew losing Daddy Joe was on the horizon. I began to notice other grandchild-grandparent relationships happening around me. Friends who visited their grandparents a few times a year, got birthday cards with five dollars folded in the crease of the card. They loved their grandparents, but there was a separation or buffer of some kind that made their relationship feel safer in the long run. They weren't intertwined with an everyday thought, a phone call, or a weekly visit. When I looked at Daddy Joe, when I heard his voice, the world was in order. The universe was unfolding as it should; everything was aligned. He was as important to me as the organs humming and working in my body. How was I supposed to even consider that this part of me would one day not exist? How do you think about the essential gears of your life tripping, locking up, failing to turn?

"When he dies, just shoot me," I told friends.

As essential as Daddy Joe was for me, he had been my mom's only parent since she had been fourteen. He was her heart, and we both loved him with a ferocity that bonded us. She was the one who kept him fed, kept him up-to-date with his doctor appointments. She was the one who found him at his worst—the one who saved him when he began to falter.

In the comic book world, death is usually followed by a resurrection explained by a misunderstanding or superhuman force that reverses the devastation. The deaths of superheroes have become so untrustworthy that readers have become numb to these "losses." It is assumed that we will be seeing this superhero again, somewhere down the line.

On March 8, 2007, the *New York Times* announced, "Captain America Is Dead; National Hero Since 1941." In *Captain America* #25, the highest-selling comic that month, Captain America was fatally shot by Sharon Carter, an intelligence agent who was romantically involved with Steve Rogers and who happened to be under the control of Dr. Faustus, a supervillain.

"It seemed a little radical when it was first brought up," Dan Buckley, the president and publisher of Marvel Entertainment, is quoted saying in the article. "But sometimes stories just take you places."

In 2009, Daddy Joe would again be interviewed about the supposed death of Captain America, this time at the Big Apple Comic Con. "He's 70 years old but . . . I get nervous when they keep trying to kill him off, but . . . people love Captain America," he said.

Since 2007 wasn't the first time Daddy Joe had received a call from the Marvel powers-that-be to let him know Cap was being offed, he took the news in stride. A few years earlier, he'd honored another rumored death by doing a painting with my aunt Gail that re-created Jesus's Last Supper. Captain America was in the center, and cheeseburgers, fries, and soda replaced the usual bread and wine.

Even though everyone knew that this couldn't possibly be the end for Captain America—there were already talks of movies, after all—I found the death unsettling. The character was a comforting, seemingly permanent mark in the world, keeping Daddy Joe secure and present. A world without Captain America made me think of a world without Daddy Joe. It reminded me of his mortality.

That year, Daddy Joe was interviewed for the show *Chasing Life* with Dr. Sanjay Gupta on CNN. When my mom and I watched the episode together, we doubled over with laughter at the B-roll shot of him walking down his block, east toward Eighth Avenue.

"Like a crab!" my mom exclaimed with a laugh.

The news anchor's voice plays over the footage: "The press has stopped this year for the patriotic cartoon Captain America after sixty-six years in print." The picture cuts to Daddy Joe sitting at his art table. "But his creator, Joe Simon, is still kicking and drawing at ninety-three. This morning, he shares his secret to healthy aging."

Daddy Joe looks up from the sketch on his table and at the camera. "Jack Kirby and I did *Captain America* for the whole of 1941. And every issue was a sellout. We were movie directors, we were the script men, we were the pencillers, we were the colorers, the inkers. Look at this." He holds up his hand, the side of it smudged with ink. "And we had dirty hands."

Dr. Gupta asked him his secret to living such a long life. I listened as if his life actually depended on it. I needed to know that he had this living thing down—even though he had already accomplished ninety-three years of it.

"My secret is work," he said. "I think it keeps my mind going. My memory is very good. I talk to my characters. It's true. You can do that. And they don't answer back a lot, but if one ever does, I know it's time to go."

I wondered if he joked about his death as a gift to the rest of us, to make his departure more tolerable, less serious. Or maybe he did it because he was truly ready to go. Either way, I hated it. The more he joked about dying, the angrier I got with him. How could he be so insensitive? How could he joke about his death like this after living through the heartbreak of losing his wife, the mother of his children? My responses to his jokes evolved from an eye roll and forced laugh to outright ignoring him. I figured if I didn't respond, or if I pretended not to hear him, the universe would do the same. He wasn't a superhero who could escape the finality of death.

TWENTY-TWO

Searching for a Love Like His—Online

2008–2009

While Daddy Joe believed that I would find someone quickly after Jake and I broke up, it was a different world than when he met Harriet, sitting behind her desk, adorable and witty. People were using the internet to find love. Waiting for the chance to meet someone out on the street, in a bar, or through a friend was becoming less and less appealing. While online dating was catching on, it carried a stigma. I browsed sites like OkCupid and Match.com, embarrassed that I wasn't meeting anyone the old-fashioned way. My friends laughed when I first told them I was using online dating, shaking their heads at my outlandish behavior. After I met two decent guys within three weeks, they all signed up and asked for help with their profiles. "It's like online shopping for guys!" I reasoned.

After nearly two months of dating Brad, I decided to confess to my mom how we met. I originally told her I'd met him through a work friend. I called her, clinging to my confidence. If she didn't approve, that was her problem.

"Mom, remember how I told you I met Brad?"

"Yeah, through Ben, that boy you worked with."

"That's not really how I met him."

"How did you meet him?" She sounded nervous.

"On an online dating website."

I was ready for the downpour of judgment and pity.

"So?" she replied. "Everyone's doing that now. I listen to Dr. Joyce Brothers on the radio. I know what's going on these days."

Dr. Joyce Brothers, who had a radio show on New York's WOR, was part of my mom's morning ritual, along with her coffee and handful of vitamins.

"Why didn't you tell me that?" she asked.

"Because there's a stigma with online dating. It's really catching on, but I feel like your generation doesn't really get it or like it."

"No, I know a lot of my friends' kids are doing it."

"Just don't tell Dad. Or anyone else in the family."

I knew she wouldn't keep this from my dad, but it was worth a shot.

"Okay."

"Mom."

"I won't!"

"Swear?"

"I won't tell him."

X

A month after my dating confession, I came home for another visit. Upon walking through the apartment door, my mom was in my face, eager to shower me with questions and show me her latest beauty product purchases. These products became something more like collector items, rarely used.

"Did my ass get too big?" she asked, twisting her body to try to catch a glimpse of herself.

My mom had always had the better body, which had been embarrassing for a teenager. Strangers had often asked if we were sisters. After my sophomore year of high school, I dropped my baby fat, losing about twenty pounds. While my friends whispered behind my back that I must have some sort of eating disorder, I figured that my mom's genes, the ones I wanted, had decided to make their presence known. I was still waiting for my dad's genes to retract my nose.

After the four-hour drive, and an additional half hour of trying to find parking for my '94 red Corolla, I just wanted to rest for bit.

"Megan, come look at this new foundation I found," my mom went on. "I swear, it makes me look twenty years old!"

"Just give me a minute," I pleaded.

I plopped down on the bed in the living room behind the sliding glass door, where my parents now slept. She followed me, holding a bag of seaweed snacks.

"Have you ever had these? I got them on sale at the health food store."

"No."

"Try one."

"No thanks." I closed my eyes.

"Did I tell you what Jillian's teacher said about her?"

"Yes."

"Megan, I was dying. She told us that—"

"You already told me!" I interrupted.

She turned around and walked away. "She's in a mood again!" she announced to the apartment.

Later that night, after I had decompressed in a scalding-hot bath and had some dinner, I found my parents, sixteen-year-old brother, and ten-year-old sister watching TV on the full-size bed behind the sliding glass door. The bed was lengthwise against the wall, couch-like.

"Move over," I told my brother, and wedged myself between the window and him. My mom rolled up her pant leg and pointed her foot high in the air.

"Look at this! A dancer! Let me see yours, Megan."

I lifted my leg, my loose pajama pants falling and bunching at my thigh. Even with my years of dance, I strained to get my foot to point as well as hers. She had high arches, but I had gotten my dad's flat feet. When I started dancing in pointe shoes at twelve years old, I knew my career was over.

The rest of the family followed her lead, comparing who was blessed with her genetics, and who had my dad's.

My mom lowered her leg. "Jillian, it's late. Time for bed."

I got up to check my email at the computer sitting in the dining room, on a long table with a printer and box of blank paper.

Once Jillian was in bed, my mom settled onto the folded futon behind me.

"Megan," she said, flossing her teeth with her legs crossed and a Patagonia catalog opened on her lap.

"What?"

"What are you doing?" she asked with her hand in her mouth.

"Looking at porn."

She laughed.

"I'm checking my email, why?"

"Show me that website for Jewish dating."

I looked at her, my eyes wide with annoyance. My dad was still on their bed, watching the news, only the half-open sliding glass door between them. I prayed he hadn't heard.

"C'mon," she said, not understanding my look, or perhaps not caring. "Let's find me a man."

"Mom!" I whined. Somehow, she could still get me to do that like I was twelve again. "You promised you wouldn't tell."

"Oh, he doesn't care." She waved, the floss swinging from her hand. She got off the couch and stood behind me. "C'mon, show me!"

I showed her the different ways you could narrow down your search: age, height, kosher or not, and so on. The results loaded on the page, and she became intrigued.

"Click on that one," she said, pointing to a narrow-headed guy.

"Ew, Mom!"

"What? What's wrong with him?"

"He's hideous."

"Just open his picture."

I did, just to show her how bad her choice was.

"Oy. That's not pretty."

"Told you." I continued scrolling down.

"He's not that bad, Megan. Is he Jewish?"

"Mom, that's the whole point of the website."

"So, he's Jewish?"

"Yes."

"Keep going."

We continued searching for a few minutes—*What's wrong with his head? Are those his ears? Only a mother could love that.* As we were picking apart a nerdy-looking guy from Brookline, my dad walked by, heading for the kitchen. I turned red. He didn't even give us a second glance, but I was ashamed. I may as well have been searching through an online penis catalog.

Then I heard my sister's footsteps come out of the bedroom. She looked wide awake and had obviously been listening to us.

"Can I look for a boyfriend, too?" she asked, a mischievous grin on her face.

"Sure, let's all find a boyfriend," my mom said, not taking her eyes off the computer screen.

I continued scrolling down the page until my mom said, "Ooh, wait! Who's that? ZestyTomato? Open his picture. Ooh, I like him!"

She looked at me, her eyes wide with excitement. My dad walked back to the living room, and my mom yelled after him.

"Papa! Come look at this one! He's perfect!"

My dad looked pissed.

"He's so jealous," she said, turning back to me.

"He's not jealous; he's ashamed that I have to resort to this." I slumped in my chair.

"No, he's jealous that I like ZestyTomato. Send ZestyTomato a message."

"I can't. I have to be a paid member."

"So pay."

"I'm not spending thirty dollars a month for this! I don't want to use this site. None of the guys are attractive."

"Megan, I love ZestyTomato! I'll pay for it! Is he Jewish?"

"Mom, they're all Jewish," Jillian said from her seat.

"Papa! Come look at this one and tell me he's not perfect!" my mom yelled across the apartment.

He answered with annoyance, "No! Who would put their picture on the internet like that?"

I looked pointedly at my mom. "See?"

"Everyone is doing it! You don't know anything. Megan, send ZestyTomato a message."

"I'm going to bed. Jill, you should go to bed, too."

I got up, Jillian following my lead.

"Jillian, go pee-pee before you go back into bed," my mom called to her as she walked toward the bedroom. "Megan."

"What?" I asked, my back to her.

"ZestyTomato."

X

Daddy Joe carried his love for Harriet long after her death, and the stories of their marriage became a fairy tale for me to compare my own love life to. I heard from friends not long after visiting my family that Jake was married.

"Do you really love me?" I had asked him once. "Like, if we broke up, would you just marry the next girl? Is that all you want?"

He had looked at me as though I were crazy, which I had started to feel I might be. His commitment had begun to feel too good to be true. I couldn't believe that someone's devotion to me could be that intense.

I didn't mind going on dates. I enjoyed talking to most of the guys I met, but even if there was a spark at that first meeting, it ultimately faded by date two or three. There were a few three-month-long relationships here and there, but it all felt forced. I began to wonder if I'd made a mistake.

TWENTY-THREE

Young Romance

2010

Ж

Daddy Joe took a bite out of a turkey and Brie sandwich, mayonnaise in the corner of his mouth. Before heading to his apartment I'd stopped at Whole Foods to buy him the sandwich and red seedless grapes.

As he got older, his protests increased. "Oh, I'm not hungry." I convinced him to take a few bites, and each time I watched with delight as he finished the whole sandwich.

On this day, along with my shopping bags, I brought my new boyfriend. He was my latest online dating success, but this one felt different. It was as if I'd found my other shoe. He fit.

I had received an email from a guy named Larry in February 2010. "I know that this process is a bit weird," he wrote. "I much would have preferred to look you in the eye and shake your hand and say the pleasure is all mine. Instead I'm typing and you're reading an email from a complete stranger."

We emailed back and forth a few times to lay down the basics: He was six years older than me, from a suburb outside of Chicago, and owned a café and bagel bakery in Boston. And the schmear on top? He was Jewish. When he asked me if I'd like to meet, I told him I'd love to and suggested my favorite coffee shop—not his—on Super Bowl Sunday at noon.

"Work is pretty busy at that time," he said. "Two thirty okay?"

I arrived at 1369 Coffee House in Central Square five minutes before we were supposed to meet, so that I could get my coffee—Colombian with extra cream—and have a moment to prep myself for another online stranger. As I waited for my order, the glass door opened, the afternoon sun blazing its way through, illuminating Larry's head. I raised my hand to identify myself.

"Hi," he said. "I'm Larry." He held out his hand, a formality that made me laugh.

"Hi. Megan."

"Well, this is awkward," he said, laughing with me.

After getting our coffees, we found a table in the back. He felt different than the others. Talking to him felt comfortable, like we knew each other already. I liked his old-school Nike sneakers, how he smelled like warm bagels. When we decided to head outside and sit on the grass of City Hall with our coffees, he said he wanted to use the bathroom preemptively. I swooned.

We talked about our long-term relationships, both of us broken by the end of them.

"It's brutal," he said, his legs outstretched in the grass. The City Hall clock tower loomed behind us.

"I'm starting to think I won't love again," I told him, shrugging as if I was comfortable with this idea. Like I had come to terms with my loveless fate.

"Oh, really?" He was amused.

Two hours later, he said he had to head back to Brookline to watch the game with his friends.

"Do you want a ride back to your apartment?" he asked.

"Are you going to murder me?"

"Well, I am driving a van. . . ."

"A van?!" I yelled in pretend fear. It was his bagel van—white, the inside cavernous and smelling of yeast. After I climbed into the pas-senger seat, he leaned over to help me figure out the seat belt.

"This is really classy, I know," he said, turning the key in the igni-tion, the van rattling to life. He pulled into the traffic of Mass Ave, taking a right toward Broadway and Inman Square, where I lived with my best friend, Nina.

In front of my apartment, he put the van in park, the floor still humming beneath our feet.

"Thanks for the ride," I said, putting the strap of my purse over my shoulder. I leaned over and gave him a hug.

"We should do this again," he said. "If you want?"

"Yeah. Definitely."

X

Four months later, I brought Larry to New York for the ultimate test.

"You have to speak loudly," I told him as we rode up the elevator to the sixth floor of Daddy Joe's building. "His hearing isn't great."

After walking through Daddy Joe's door, I saw the apartment from the perspective of a stranger—the sounds of a Syracuse University bas-ketball game, the comic book art on the walls that made him different from other grandfathers. I usually waited to drop his name, his cre-ations, into conversations with the guys I liked. Larry was the first guy I'd dated since Jake to meet him, to be welcomed into the warmth of his small apartment—my secret hideaway.

As they talked, Daddy Joe regaling Larry with stories of the comic business and Larry asking the appropriate amount of questions, I was grateful for how Larry spoke to him. He kept his voice loud enough to hear but didn't speak to him like he was losing his marbles. At one point, Larry looked at me quickly, probably trying to make me laugh over a double entendre of some kind—it was really hard, Megan wasn't easy—and Daddy Joe stopped midsentence.

"What?" he asked.

Taken aback, Larry started to laugh uncomfortably.

"Oh, I get it," Daddy Joe said, smiling slyly. "You can't get anything by old Joe, you know."

Larry quickly learned that Daddy Joe was still sharp as a tack.

Eventually, Larry stood up to study the artwork on the walls. "This is great," he said, pointing at two framed pieces placed side by side. One was a self-portrait of Daddy Joe finishing the boot of one of the Newsboy Legion boys and surrounded by other characters, and the other depicted even more of his popular characters. "Is this you?"

Daddy Joe pushed back in his chair a bit, making it tilt toward the corner of the room with the TV. "Yes, I gave myself a nose job."

"Who is this? Obviously not Captain America, right?" Larry pointed to a patriotic-looking superhero—his chest also red, white, and blue, with a star—standing in the back of the crowd.

"Fighting American," Daddy Joe said, enjoying the questions. "Kirby and I did that one after we found out Timely-Atlas was bringing back Captain America." Timely-Atlas was what Marvel was at that time.

It had been 1953 when they heard the news that Cap was coming back. Daddy Joe refused to let his old employer corner the market on patriotism, so the duo thought up Fighting American. Instead of fighting Nazis, he would protect the country from more timely threats, like communism. The new Captain America series died after only three issues, and Fighting American lasted seven. Victory was theirs.

I got up to pour myself a glass of root beer in the kitchen. I watched the two of them talk, the refrigerator emitting a low buzzing sound behind me—Daddy Joe, my past, my foundation, evaluating my possible future.

Daddy Joe looked at me in the kitchen, and then back at Larry. "You know, I raised Megan," Daddy Joe told him.

"I heard," Larry said, and looked at me curiously, as if I were one of Daddy Joe's creations. As if I should've been in the painting on the wall, adorned in a colorful costume. We all studied one another—all of us trying to figure out how we could fit, *if* we would all fit together.

TWENTY-FOUR

Ninety-Eight Candles

2011

Ж

"Want to run over to Crumbs Bake Shop and order him a birthday cake?" my mom asked later that month, while I was home for another visit.

I obliged, telling the bakery that we needed the Captain America shield on top of a cake. I knew they assumed it was for a child's birthday, not for the almost ninety-eight-year-old creator of Captain America. I found a small thrill in my secret mission.

With cake in hand, my brother, sister, mom, cousin Emily, and I met at Daddy Joe's apartment the next afternoon. He clapped his hands with delight when he saw the cake and exclaimed, "That's wonderful!" It was a round vanilla cake topped with the red, white, and blue Captain America shield. Daddy Joe was wearing a Heroes Convention T-shirt from 2006 with Captain America on it.

His video camera was long retired by this time, so Emily used her smartphone to record the lighting of the cake.

"How old are you?" she asked him once she started recording.

"Ninety-eight!" he exclaimed, his elbow resting on the arm of his chair. I was behind him, lighting the candles on the cake that sat on his drawing table. "Ninety-eight today!" he added.

"Tomorrow!" Emily corrected him with a smile. "Okay, blow out the candles."

"Oh, okay." He swiveled the chair around to face the cake. "Emily, you should be over here with the camera." He directed her to stand in front of him to get the best shot. After she got into position, he paused. "The old man's still working!"

He held up a rough painting of Captain America charging through a glass window. The blue of his shield bled into the white of the star, the background a smudge of yellow paint. The caption above Cap's head read, "You sent for me, President Roosevelt?"

"Ninety-eight and still working!" he repeated. The candles were starting to melt onto themselves, threatening to solidify on the frosting.

I couldn't help but notice the difference in his work, the details of Captain America's body and face looser, less defined. The fatigue of his hand starting to show on the page. He turned the painting around to show the head of Captain America. He held it over his face.

"Okay, blow them out!" I called from off-camera. "Before they melt all the way down."

"Oh, okay." He put it down, scooching closer to the art table. Picking up his coffee cup, he went for a sip, and then remembered the candles again. "Okay, you want me to blow this out?"

"Make a wish and blow them out," I said, trying not to sound impatient. The melting candles started to feel like the clock counting down on a bomb.

He leaned forward, took a breath in, and then stopped. "Old cigar-smoking Joe," he said. And then began to sing, "Cigar-smoking Joe! Cigar-smoking Joe! He's gonna blow out ninety-eight candles! Nintey-eight candles . . . !"

"The cake is going to melt!"

". . . Old smoking Joe, watch this!" He leaned forward again, this time filling his lungs, and blew a strong wind over the candles, extinguishing each one.

"Wow!" my mom exclaimed from the futon.

He looked up at the camera, pleased and amazed with himself. "What power!" He reached for his sandwich and took a big bite.

Emily put down her phone.

"Do you want a piece of cake now?" I asked.

"Just a little one. I'm not that hungry," he said. I cut him a big, thick piece and placed it in front of him.

"Did you see the book?" he asked, talking about his memoir *My Life in Comics*, which had been published a few months earlier. He had spent a year writing it, and knowing that I wanted a career in editing and writing, he allowed me to serve as consulting editor. I was an administrative assistant in Harvard's Department of Anthropology by day and reading Word documents sent over by Daddy Joe's editor at night. I enjoyed the task of editing but was even happier to learn more about Daddy Joe in those pages.

"Yeah, it looks great," I said.

"*Yes*," he corrected as he took a bite of cake. "I'm a writer, too, you know."

Later, before we headed home, my brother, sister, and I headed up to the roof, the ground covered in small pebbles that rolled and knocked together under our feet. The wind was as strong as ever. I looked out over the railing, down at the other rooftops.

Daddy Joe was too weak to climb the steps up to the roof door. I thought of him still sitting in his chair and how he wouldn't be going on a rooftop adventure with me again. It didn't feel right being up there, so close to the sky, without him.

I knew that this could be his last birthday, so when he blew out the candles on his small red, white, and blue shield cake, I studied him intently. That scene—the O of his mouth, his hands pushing against the leather chair for leverage—was saved in my brain as a token of survival. I needed it in order to begin the journey of losing him.

X

After Daddy Joe had his stroke, the doctors ordered an MRI.

"Well, Mr. Simon," the on-duty doctor told him, "let's just say you're never going senile. Everything looks great."

Daddy Joe told this story from behind a table at the 2011 New York Comic Con, a few days after I headed back to Boston. He was the star of the panel, sitting with his editor, Steve; my sister, now thirteen, seated beside him; and my cousin Emily next to her. It was a few days after his ninety-eighth birthday and as he was pushed to the stage in a wheelchair, the crowd sang "Happy Birthday."

"So, after the doctor told me this," he continued, "I decided I should write my memoir."

"He holds this MRI over all of us," his editor said with a laugh. "He's going to outlast us all."

While he was in the hospital, word got around about who he was. The nurses stood in a line to get a drawing and autograph. He spent his first day in the hospital sharing a room with other patients, one of them a man who, according to Daddy Joe, didn't have any underwear.

"I told the nurses to give him my dessert. He didn't even have underwear! When I made a sketch for him, I wrote, 'To my friend,' because I didn't know his name. That set him off. He sat there and cried."

Daddy Joe continued, with low grumbles between bouts of long pauses as he tried to think of his next point, talking about creating the Red Skull, and what it was like to work in the comic business during the Golden Age.

"Stan Lee first worked for you and Jack, right?" his editor asked. "Can you tell us a little about that?"

"Stan Lee's a good guy." Daddy Joe paused, thumping his cane to the floor. "I made him what he is today."

TWENTY-FIVE

Hanging On

2011

Ж

I called Daddy Joe on my way home from work a few weeks after his birthday. These were usually quick conversations, in which he'd give me the rundown of his latest art projects or annoyances with a son, daughter, or business acquaintance. He had visitors coming frequently, tiring him out, but keeping his mind sharp—the reminiscing of comic days gone by, the talk of business.

"Harry's here. He's scanning everything from the file cabinet in my bedroom."

That was where all his old artwork was kept, a gold mine of collectible covers, original pages, and re-creations. Harry was a comics historian, author, and collector who had become close with Daddy Joe over the years.

"How are you feeling?" I asked him. He'd been falling in the middle of the night, a new bruise on him each time my mom came downtown.

"I'm ready to go," he told me.

I didn't respond.

"Your mother wants me to get a visiting nurse," he continued.

"And how do you feel about that?"

"I don't need anyone. I'll be gone soon anyway."

"I think it's a good idea," I said.

My mom found a woman named Helena to clean and cook for Daddy Joe a few times a week. She wasn't a nurse, but she came recommended from a friend. She was hardworking and kind.

"She's too damn loud," Daddy Joe complained to my mom. But over the next month or so, he began to find comfort in Helena's presence. He teased her, gave her shit, but in a way that meant that he enjoyed her company.

One afternoon, Helena arrived agitated. She went straight for his kitchen to start cleaning. "Hi, Mr. Simon," she said, scrubbing a pan vigorously.

He was at his kitchen table reading his *New York Post* and drinking his second cup of coffee. Placing the cup on the blondwood table, he watched her attack the dishes with an unusual force.

"That doorman," she said, moving on to the stained coffeepot, "was trying to get my phone number."

"Who? José?"

"Whatever his name is. Wouldn't let up."

Daddy Joe pushed back his chair, sliding it against the parquet floor, and, with some effort, lifted himself up to standing. Helena stopped scrubbing and turned off the water.

"Where are you going?"

"To have a little chat with José."

"Mr. Simon, sit down."

He ignored her, leaning forward to help his momentum, and headed out the door. She followed him down the popcorn-walled hallway and into the elevator.

"What are you going to do? This is ridiculous."

"Don't worry about it," he said, the elevator doors opening at the lobby.

She watched him charge to the doorman's desk with a renewed energy.

"What are you doing down here?" he asked the doorman. "Playing with yourself?"

Daddy Joe seemed to hit a stride with his new life of nurses and help. Where once our visits had been interrupted by guys in the comic book business, it was now women with knowing smiles and secrets to tell the family—he tried to sneak a pill, we found candy in this drawer.

That year, during a visit to New York for Thanksgiving, I found him on his bed, rifling through his dresser drawers.

"Hi, Daddy Joe," I said, walking into his bedroom.

"Where are my pills?" he asked, not looking at me.

"I don't know. I'll ask the nurse." She was a new one, someone to fill in on the days that Helena couldn't come. I found her sitting at his desk chair, looking at her phone.

"He's looking for his pills. Do you know which ones he means?"

She looked up from her phone. "He's not allowed to have any more today. He already had two."

"God damn it, where are my pills?" Daddy Joe hollered from his bedroom, his anger making my limbs feel weightless.

"She said you already had two today. You can't take too much," I explained calmly, willing him back to his jovial self.

"Bullshit. Why is everyone hiding my medicine?"

He looked at me like I was the enemy.

My mom had been crying for years that his health was deteriorating, but I'd accused her of being dramatic. I wouldn't believe it—couldn't believe it—even if he was in his nineties. As he yelled from his bedroom, the air in his apartment seemed to be charged differently, the fading energy of his final days.

After I left his apartment, I met some friends in Central Park and cried on a large gray rock as the sun set behind midtown.

"It wasn't him," I told my friends. "That wasn't him."

A week later, Daddy Joe and I spoke on the phone during my lunch break. I leaned against the wall of Harvard's Memorial Chapel.

"Listen," he said. "I need a website. It needs to be copyright of Joseph H. Simon."

"Okay," I said, eager for the task. I was taking an intro to web coding class at the Harvard Extension School. It was meant to supplement the work I was doing as a communications assistant, but I was ready to take my newfound skills outside of work. "I'm learning Photoshop, so I can get some nice designs. Maybe a collage of comic book covers," I offered.

"Cool. Just make sure it says 'All rights reserved.'"

He sounded like himself. I figured that what I had seen a few weeks earlier was only a fluke in his system, something like his crappy computer that froze up on a daily basis.

I got to work, asking Harry the comic historian to send me some scans and high-res images to use as a header for the homepage. I added a contact form that soon opened the floodgates for interview and signing requests.

Daddy Joe's eagerness to continue working comforted and fueled me to help. As long as he was excited to be present, I knew that all was right in the world.

〤

I decided to start another new project. "I've got a great idea," I told him in an email. "I'm going to take your romance covers and put them on T-shirts."

The covers were retro enough and the dialogue corny enough to be appealing: "I guess I was jealous of my own Aunt! That's why I swore to get even when she told me I was . . . BOY CRAZY."

I used my basic Photoshop skills to get the images just right and hired a local T-shirt printer in Somerville to print a few sample shirts. At the factory, with the machines thumping, I removed the shirts from a paper bag and ran my hand over the images. I was proud of my work, excited to show Daddy Joe.

Earlier that month, I had forwarded Larry an email from Groupon for a boudoir photo shoot. "For Hanukkah?" I joked.

But Larry thought it was a serious request, and a few hours later, he forwarded me the confirmation email for his purchase.

I immediately called him from my desk at work. "What the fuck?" I asked. "You thought I was serious?"

"Yes! I don't know!" He began to laugh.

With my forehead in my palm, I thought of something. "Wait. Maybe I can use this to get photos of me in the T-shirts."

"See? It *is* a good present!" Larry said, relieved.

I met the photographers at Hotel Marlowe in Cambridge, which overlooked the Boston skyline. They knew I was wearing my creations instead of taking anything off, and they agreed to do a few shots of the T-shirts alone, neatly fanned out on the bed. I would use the photos for an Etsy page.

I got the final, edited photos on December 12 and sent an email to the family. "These are the best of the bunch. I'm so excited to finally have the photos of them. Emily, can you show Daddy Joe these on his computer?"

"They look great! Yes, I'll show him tomorrow," she responded. She was in between jobs, living in the city, and helping out with Daddy Joe a few times a week.

But she couldn't make it to his apartment the next day. She promised to show him the day after.

TWENTY-SIX

The Inevitable

December 14, 2011

✕

As Daddy Joe sat on the edge of his unmade bed, his heart stopped during a pneumonia-induced coughing fit.

I was washing my hair in the Brookline apartment I shared with Larry. As the hot water chased the shampoo suds from my hair, Daddy Joe was leaving this world.

I saw the missed call when I got out of the shower, and listened to the message left by my uncle while sitting on Larry's blue couch, my hair dripping down my back and darkening the towel wrapped around my chest. The moment the words "heart gave out" entered my ear and registered in my brain, my hand clamped over my mouth. I sat there, staring at a dark TV screen that reflected my image back to me. There I was, losing him. This is what I looked like losing him.

Larry was in the shower, but I had to tell him that instant. I didn't want to hold it by myself any longer—I didn't feel capable of that. I burst into the bathroom.

"He's dying," I said to the steam.

"What?" Larry asked, sliding open the shower's glass door.

"Daddy Joe. He's in the hospital. This is it."

I was close to hyperventilating. Larry turned off the water, wrapped a towel around his waist, and stepped out over the tub.

"What should I do?" I asked him.

"Get on the next train and go see him."

"He's not conscious." I looked down, noticed I was still in a wet towel, and decided I needed to be dressed for a situation this upsetting. A towel was unacceptable.

"Get on the next train and be by his side," Larry said as I threw clothes on my body. "Say goodbye."

A part of me, a large part of me—the selfish part?—didn't want to go. There was a magnetic pull trying to keep me in that apartment in order to avoid the truth of what was happening. If I didn't go to New York, if I didn't see him in the hospital bed, then none of this would be real. But Larry's insistence got me out the door and into his Prius.

An hour later, I was at South Station, trying not to sob while I bought my one-way train ticket to Penn Station. *A ticket to go watch Daddy Joe die*, I thought. As the train pulled away from the station, the scenery moving faster, blurring in the late-morning sun, I called my mom.

"Megan," she moaned.

All we could do for the first few minutes of the phone call was cry. What else was there to do? After we both caught our breaths, she told me that my dad was at the hospital.

"He's on life support. He never wanted that. I want to take him off." Daddy Joe never wanted to be resuscitated, and it pained my mom to think of him in the hospital bed, his heart beating fake thumps of life.

But on the train, I was overtaken with an urgency to see him one last time while he was still alive. Even if it wasn't real, even if he was empty.

"I don't want him to die while I'm sitting on this train," I whimpered into the phone as a businessman across the aisle nervously glanced over.

My mom stayed uptown, lying on my brother's bed, heartbroken, waiting for it to be over. She had lost her mother at such a young age;

Daddy Joe was her everything. She had loved him for almost sixty years and now knew that the time had come. She would be without both parents.

I learned that we all need different things in our time of grief. I found myself on a mission to see him one last time, and she didn't want her last memory to be of him motionless, tubes going in and out of him. I never questioned her choice to stay under that blanket, her Maine coon cat probably curled up at her feet.

The train couldn't move fast enough. There was an hourglass over-turned in my head, and with each granule of sand that dropped, my anxiety soared. What if I didn't make it in time? What if I'd never be near his living body again? I secured a place at the doors of the train before we even entered the tunnel into Penn Station and leapt out the moment they opened, the old plastic wheels of my suitcase half drag-ging and half rolling behind me.

In front of me was a student from the Department of Anthropology where I worked.

"Hi!" he said cheerfully. "What are you doing in New York?"

"My grandfather is in the hospital," I told him, barely stopping. "I'm sorry, I can't talk."

"Oh. I'm so sorry," I heard him say behind me as I ran toward the staircase.

My dad stood guard at the hospital, talking with doctors, wel-coming family members. Right before my arrival, he ran out to make some calls to work, and because I was terrified to see Daddy Joe with all the tubes and machinery, I waited in the hall until he was able to go in the room with me. I was five years old again, scared and waiting for my dad to hold my hand.

"Okay, you ready?" he asked after he returned. We stood outside the doorway of the dark room. The nurses were busy at their station behind us. I didn't answer, just walked in.

Keeping my gaze on the hospital window overlooking the night filled with lit-up buildings, I walked directly to the chair beside his bed. My dad stood beside me as I put my hand on top of Daddy Joe's, my eyes fixed to my lap. Beneath my palm, I felt his wrinkles and rough skin, the warmth of his body. Beneath my fingers were his fingers, long, elegant. I thought about the fact that he would never hold a paintbrush again.

As the machines beeped and whirred, my dad, with his usual strength and comfort, spoke about the peaceful finality of his father's death twenty-five years earlier. I nodded as he spoke, trying to find acceptance through his words, trying to feed off his strength.

"I think the rabbi is here. I'll be right back," he said, leaving me alone with the sounds of the machines.

I still couldn't look directly at Daddy Joe, or speak to him, knowing that the words would get caught in my throat. Instead, I leaned over and kissed him on the cheek, as I had done so many times before. Only this time, it was unreciprocated. It was hollow and yet far too weighted. I knew this was the last kiss on the cheek that I would ever give him. I felt sick. It was everything I had dreaded for decades all wrapped up into one moment—dark and silent, except for the steady beeps.

A strange figure entered the room—the rabbi, the shadow of his hat, a tall *shtreimel*, making his entrance that much more dramatic. An entrance that Daddy Joe would have preferred.

After taking Daddy Joe off life support, the doctor spoke with family members in the painfully bright hallway. We were told it could take hours for him to pass, so my dad, my cousin Emily, and I went across the street to get some dinner at a Greek restaurant. I didn't have an appetite, only a raging headache that I forced lemon potatoes into my mouth to cure. I called Larry from outside the restaurant and thanked him for getting me on the train, for making sure that I got to say goodbye, or at least be by his side before he died.

"Do you think he knows that I was there?" I asked.

"I'm sure of it. Just let me know when I should head down there, okay?"

An hour later, the three of us headed back to the hospital, ready for the wait. But as we walked down the hallway toward Daddy Joe's room, my uncle turned to us from the doorway. And I knew. It was in the air, in the city. He was gone.

My brother was in college in Maine and planned to take a bus into the city the next day. I slept in his bed that night, waking frequently, remembering where I was, why I was there, that Daddy Joe was gone. My mom was on the other side of the wall, drowning in grief.

TWENTY-SEVEN

Goodbye, for Now

2011

Ж

Shock is an invaluable human response. I went through the motions of the next few days in a robotic state; helping to pick out a wooden casket, finding a rabbi who would preside over the funeral on a Friday afternoon, and refereeing the fight to bury him in a suit—which he hated—or his favorite Captain America shirt. It was decided that his Captain America shirt would go under the suit.

He was buried on the outer edges of a graveyard on Long Island, a busy road and gas station within view. A place I would never want to return, but it was where Harriet was buried and waiting for him to join her.

I made it through the car ride to his funeral with the help of an Imodium my mom gave me, my stomach a reliable indicator of my mental state. Larry drove me while my parents, brother, and sister went in their '98 Volvo. I was grateful for the silent ride as I watched the city turn to Queens and then Long Island.

As we pulled into the cemetery, driving slowly down a long path bordered by headstones, I looked for a bathroom.

"Over there," I said, pointing. Larry made a right, following my directions. My eyes landed on my aunt Gail's car.

"There's Gail!" I exclaimed. With an immediate and urgent need to get to her, I went for the door handle.

"Wait!" Larry yelled. "Let me stop the car first!"

I was already out and heading for her. We made eye contact from across the lot, and although we're not a family to show physical affection, I threw my arms around her. I wanted to cling to someone else who felt murdered by Daddy Joe's death, and Gail was an easier, less-complicated target than my mom.

At the grave site, family and friends were gathered, dressed in black and speaking in soft voices.

"You have diarrhea, Megan?" a family friend announced to the crowd as we waited for the hearse to arrive. Apparently along with my grandfather's death, the topic of the morning was my bowel movements.

"Uh, yeah." I murmured, and walked away to deal with something more traumatizing, like the casket arriving.

Our family turned to watch the hearse pull up to the grave site. I was in a crowd, but the moment his casket was pulled from the back of the car, I was alone, thrust into a black hole—the other faces and voices fading into blobs of sound and color.

"I can't do this," I told Larry as I walked away toward his Prius. I shut the driver's-side door and closed my eyes for a moment, then reopened them. I focused on the dashboard, with all its buttons and dusty plastic, escaping the large casket being carried to its final resting place. I breathed in deeply, exhaling so that the cloud of hot air collided with the windshield. I knew I had to get back out there, to sit in the front row of folding chairs.

I took my place next to my mom, my aunt Gail beside her; with their curls and their hands folded on their laps, even their sorrow was identical. I wished I could hold some of the sorrow for them, but I could barely hold my own. The rabbi spoke, his words arcing out over our solemn faces.

At the end of the service, family members took turns putting rocks on the headstone. The fresh dirt from the grave was in a mound, waiting to be shoveled over the casket—loose and soft, like freshly ground coffee. Harriet's headstone stood beside his, the sounds of traffic on the other side of the wire fence, the pile of rocks threatening to topple over.

X

A few weeks after the funeral, the family gathered to clean out Daddy Joe's apartment. My mom, brother, sister, and I rode up in the elevator together, a small clump walking down the carpeted hallway. The closer we came to his door, the shorter my breaths became. *This is worse than watching his casket being lowered into the ground,* I thought. As my mom turned the key in the lock, I tried to prepare myself for what lay beyond the door. Or, rather, what wasn't there.

I'd never felt a room so empty.

Though filled with his stuff, sunlight, and floating dust motes, the void was unbearable. I ran to the bathroom to regain my strength, to have a moment alone with his absurdly old toiletries, the baby powder bottle turned yellow. I looked in the mirror and saw that my eyes were red. The only things left of him were his belongings and the chalky smell of his shower. His bed was still pushed from the wall, crooked, from when the paramedics rushed in to resuscitate him.

All of his artwork would be collected and put in a safe place, but the rest of it—papers, candy, art supplies, photos, VHS tapes, clothing— would be taken or tossed. It was a "potluck," as he'd said in the old home video where he jokingly detailed what should happen after his death. I looked around, trying to figure out what to take home. I was falling down a rabbit hole, trying to grab what I could: a couple of paintbrushes, the handles stained with layers of color; an old ink jar that he used to ink thousands of comics; a few photos, including the blown-up copy of my Harvard ID (I worked there, but he liked to tell people I was "at Harvard"); and the green, glow-in-the-dark flashlight I'd given him one year for his birthday.

More family arrived, armed with trash bags, pausing to look at unearthed photos or pieces of art that had been forgotten in a random drawer. His art table was already gone, so I took a seat next the taboret, the floor dusty, lined with years of cigar ash and bits of shredded eraser. I opened the small door of the taboret and found what looked like an eyeglass holder. It was rough and worn, the black lining chipping off in small pieces. Inside, I found an old Paasche airbrush. It was metal, with a small cup—almost resembling a pipe—meant to hold ink. I ran my finger over it, feeling the history, the years of creation this small tool produced. I tried to feel the ghost of his hand.

My mom was throwing papers from under his computer table into a trash bag.

"Can I keep this?" I asked her. The deal was that each grandchild could take a couple of things home with them, but we had to check with one of the parents first.

My mom barely looked at the airbrush in my hand. "Yes."

I closed the container, letting the round top of it settle into my palm.

My aunt Missy came over to me, putting her hand on my shoulder. "You okay, sweetie?" she asked. "I know this must be hard on you."

I nodded, thankful for her acknowledgment. He wasn't my father, and since his death, I'd been battling the guilt of my overwhelming heartbreak. Was it justified to feel as though my world had lost something as important as gravity or oxygen? I had thought that the death of a grandparent was responded to with a functional sadness followed by a day or two of mourning. The grief would quickly dissolve, hidden within the events of your everyday life. On top of that, he had five children of his own, as well as one great love of his life. I was one of eight grandchildren. Wasn't the proof in the numbers? I was one of many, our love diluted.

When we were done cleaning, I left his apartment for the last time. I walked out onto the street, his building, my escapes, forever behind me.

X

Afterward, I met Nina, my old roommate from Boston, who now lived in New York, down near Union Square, pulling my suitcase behind me. The plan was for both of us to have a session with a spiritual medium that she had found through a friend, and then head to her apartment in Astoria for the night. I'd escape New York the next morning and head back to Boston.

Nina went first, emerging from the room teary-eyed and smiling. Her grandmother had made an appearance, and her favorite dog from childhood, Willie, had sat on her lap. She took my seat in the waiting room as I headed to the room where the medium was waiting for me.

"Someone's here with us," she said after I got settled.

The room was dark, and I sat across a table from her. I'd given her only my first name.

"They're calling you baby. Baby girl?"

I hadn't expected to remain dry-eyed, but I was still raw from cleaning out his apartment, and so I started to cry within two minutes of the thirty-minute session.

"This person is saying that 'she's mine,'" she continued.

I nodded. Daddy Joe had used to joke to my mom that I was really his child because of all the financial help he provided for my schooling and summer camps. But I was his—regardless of and beyond all that.

The medium rattled off questions, some of them not meaning much. Each time she asked me a question that didn't spark anything, I began to lose hope that this was real, feeling that he was slipping through my fingers, leaving for good.

"I don't know if this is him, but did someone die of bad blood?

Leukemia? This is family. He's trying to say who he's with: Ronald? Robin? Was there a fluid buildup? Pneumonia? Seven? July mean something?"

His mother's name was Rose, but I didn't say this. The medium was starting to lose me, and perhaps she knew this, because she fired with, "He's standing behind you."

I smiled, not because I believed her but because I liked the idea of this. I wanted to defy science and nature and have him back.

"I can see the light move—his hand is on your shoulder. Did you feel your hair move? He's lifting up your hair—likes your hair. He said he's always by your side."

I didn't feel my hair move. I wished with all my might that I did. But I still imagined him standing behind me. I allowed myself to live in that world, if only for a moment.

Daddy Joe had once told me that when Harriet was really sick, her mother burned things in their bedroom's fireplace. "Sort of like witchcraft to make her better," he said.

I'd shaken my head, pitying Dinah—her sorrow, the level of her desperation pushing her to rely on magic or whatever spirits were in the universe to save her daughter. But sitting across from the medium, I understood Dinah more than ever. It was an attempt to gain some control over her loss. Terrible things couldn't possibly just happen without some effort to reverse them. For me, this visit was an attempt to prove that the universe hadn't permanently removed him from my life.

"Did he really like comics?" the medium continued. "I'm seeing flashes of cartoons."

I nodded, because that was all I could do after sitting for twenty minutes, praying for a sign that he was there. And this was my sign, right? How could she possibly know that he was a cartoonist? I granted myself permission to feel relief.

I spent a restless night on Nina's couch, her cat meowing every time

I rolled over. While Nina slept soundly in her bed a few feet away, I replayed my afternoon. Saying goodbye to Daddy Joe and his apartment, and then desperately trying to find him somewhere in the ether. I wondered if he was still with me at that moment or if he'd gotten too annoyed with the needy cat at my feet.

My visit to the medium was the beginning of a continuing search for him. I was a stubborn person, and now I refused to accept that he was really gone. If he wasn't in this world physically, I had to believe that he was here spiritually.

When I did sleep, it was a half sleep that resulted in a foggy head all the next day. But even with my exhaustion, both physical and emotional, I didn't sleep on the train. I rested my head against the scratched window, focusing on the passing scenery and then letting it go out of focus.

TWENTY-EIGHT

Sightings

2012

⋊

Seated in a leather massage chair, the gears rolling over my neck muscles, a woman cleaned the underside of my big toenail. When I returned to Massachusetts, I decided to treat myself to a pedicure, give myself a distraction, a treat for surviving what I thought I never could. Soon she was rubbing lotion on my calves and over my feet, running her knuckles against the arch of my foot. I closed my eyes, focusing on the *good* feelings, so different from the sorrow that I'd been carrying with me.

When the technician was done massaging and moved on to painting my nails, I opened a *People* magazine on my lap. Celebrity gossip was an easy distraction from my own world. I flipped the pages, landing on announcements: who gave birth, who got married, who died.

"Joe Simon, a Creator of Captain America, Is Dead at 98."

Dead. Is Dead.

I caught the gasp that tried to escape from my mouth, hoping it sounded like a hiccup instead. The technician looked up at me, concerned, and then back to my toes.

There were reminders of him everywhere. They were constant. While I wanted the world to know that he was missing, to understand what an integral person had been lost, I also wanted to keep the grief for myself. I wanted to store it under my sweater, to mourn him privately, fully.

After I returned to my regular life, trying to find solid ground again, the Captain America sightings became more frequent. Of course, the T-shirts had been there all along, but his absence from the world gave them more power. Each sighting stung a bit, and with that an urgency to let everyone know who he was.

"I like your shirt," I told a man in Whole Foods.

He looked down, putting his hand on the shield. "Oh, thanks."

Before he could continue his search for the perfect banana, I asked, "Do you know who created Captain America?"

He looked at me, his smile turning into a look of concentration. "Stan Lee?"

"No, no! Joe Simon and Jack Kirby. Remember that, okay?"

"Really? Joe Simon and Jack Kirby. Got it."

I walked away, leaving him to probably mutter, "What the fuck?" to the bananas.

Only a year earlier, I represented Daddy Joe with his other grandchildren at the *Captain America: The First Avenger* movie premiere in Los Angeles. Even though he was alive for the release of the movie, he was ninety-seven and too weak to make the trip from New York. A group of grandchildren scoured the internet for cheap plane tickets and hotel rooms in order to take advantage of Marvel's offer of passes. The girls in our fancy dresses and the boys in their suits met at the red-carpet entrance, where we were greeted by a Marvel representative. A film crew interviewed each of us for the movie's Blu-ray extras.

As the movie's actors made their way down the red carpet, they were cheered by fans behind the metal barriers, but we knew the real star was Daddy Joe. The movie wouldn't even exist without him. Our pride in what he'd done helped us approach actors and inform them of who he was. We were his small army, riding high.

Before we entered the theater, I pulled out my phone. "Let's call him," I said. I dialed the phone number forever emblazoned in my brain and put the phone on speaker. He answered after the third ring.

"Hi, Daddy Joe!" I yelled over the screaming fans. "We're on the red carpet!"

"You're where?" he asked. "I can barely hear you."

"The red carpet. At the premiere!" I yelled closer to the phone's microphone.

"Oh! Great! How is it?"

"Good! Can you hear everyone cheering?"

My cousin was telling the crowd closest to us to give a shout for Captain America's creator.

"It's so loud!" he said, laughing.

After we hung up the phone, we took a photo with Chris Evans in front of the large Captain America shield at the end of the red carpet, maybe fifty feet tall, and then made our way into the theater.

"Oh my god," my sister said, tugging on my arm nodding her chin toward another actor.

"Go say hello," I said.

"You do it," she whispered as he made his way closer to us.

Once he was beside us, I waved my hand.

"Sorry," he said, attempting to continue on his way.

"My sister is a huge fan," I said. "Would you be willing to take a photo with her?"

I was about to explain who our grandfather was, maybe a good enough reason for him to take a moment to slow his pace.

"I really have to go," he said, visibly annoyed.

"Great, thanks a lot," I said sarcastically.

He stopped and turned toward me. "Excuse me?"

I turned away, dragging my sister toward the bins of free popcorn and laughing.

"Only you would get in a fight with a famous actor," she said, her

face bright red from her LA sunburn and the excitement of the premiere.

We settled into our seats and the screen came alive, red- and orange-
tinted comic book panels—an arm holding a shield, a body leaping, an
explosion—rolling in fast motion. These images, or maybe seeing them
so big on the movie screen, hit me square in the chest. Comic book art
was so ingrained in me, as much a part of me as my blue eyes, that it
felt like seeing Daddy Joe's face on the screen. This was him. This was
who he was—large, colorful, exciting.

Daddy Joe watched the film at a New York screening. Even with the
close proximity to his apartment, it was still a journey for him, and he
accepted the offer of a car service and wheelchair to get there. There
had been other Captain America films, but this was different. This
was Hollywood-big, and he was thrilled, muttering, "Huh, so clever,"
during a few scenes.

I can't imagine what it was like for him, this boy from the small
city of Rochester. He saw his first "talking picture" in 1927 at the age
of fourteen—*The Jazz Singer*, starring Al Jolson and May McAvoy,
black-and-white and beyond anyone's imagination. He remembered
the audience being questioned by a crowd outside the theater afterward. *Is it true that the screen is talking and playing music?* Now
ninety-seven, he was watching his creation on a movie screen, far
more advanced in technology—the sound, the colors, the action. How
surreal it must have been for him.

We stayed in our seats as the credits rolled in the El Capitan Theatre.
We were waiting to see his name, to see credit given where it was due.
Finally, it appeared: "Based on the Marvel Comics character by Joe
Simon and Jack Kirby." We hooted and hollered, despite the looks
from those seated next to us.

X

Weeks after my pedicure, Larry and I walked down Harvard Avenue in Brookline's Coolidge Corner. The sadness had taken a permanent seat on my shoulders, and I wondered if it would ever leave. I hoped that it would one day slide gracefully down my back, never to be seen again.

Loud music jumped and reverberated out of the local synagogue, luring us up the steep steps to peek in through the windows. Larry led me by my hand, a wordless plea to focus on something other than my sorrow. Standing on my toes, I was able to see through the narrow window to the synagogue's reception hall. We watched children dancing, moving in circles, linking arms, spinning and hopping from one foot to the other—happy. As they spun and bounced, a little boy turned toward the door, revealing a Captain America T-shirt. I held my breath. But instead of letting it push the sorrow down harder onto my shoulders, I acknowledged his appearance.

Hi, Daddy Joe, I said to myself. *I miss you.*

"Hi, baby," I heard him say back. For a moment, I felt something resembling peace before my brain weaseled its way back to sorrow. But it was something, a taste of what his memory—these sightings—could mean. There was beauty beneath the sorrow.

I busied myself with work, my Harvard Extension classes, and playing house with Larry. One evening, after making salmon with asparagus and roasted potatoes, I pulled a lighter from the kitchen drawer to light a perfumed candle to mask the lingering fish smell. Running my thumb against the top of the red, plastic lighter, against the round metal gear that lit the flint, I thought of Daddy Joe and his cigars. I thought about lighting his cigar, how I looked forward to the task, waiting for him to pull a new one from his wooden humidor. I remembered the feel of his boxy lighters, heavy and cold in my hand, how he eyed me as the flame licked the end of the cigar.

"Your mother says you're a pyro," he would say, the smoke escaping from his mouth as he spoke. "Okay, that's enough."

He'd pull back from the lighter, and I'd release my thumb from the gas, flipping the lid of the lighter shut with a *clank*.

As I lit the candle, the smell of fish quickly intertwining with sandalwood, I thought of him laughing and saying, "Give me that lighter. Enough with the fire."

I placed it back in the drawer.

"Want to watch *Lost*?" Larry called from the TV room.

"Yeah, let me just—"

A loud *pop* from the drawer interrupted me. I found the lighter, blackened and smoldering. "Oh my god," I muttered. I was sure it was Daddy Joe letting me know he was there—telling me to stop playing with lighters, just as he had when I was a child.

TWENTY-NINE

New York Comic Con

2012

Ж

That summer, my mom called and asked if I'd consider sitting on the "Joe Simon Memorial Celebration" panel at the 2012 New York Comic Con.

"No way," I said. "Besides, I don't know enough about the comic business."

"That doesn't matter!" I heard her shuffling papers, probably paying bills. "You're so good with this kind of stuff."

I emotionally—and physically—couldn't do it. The idea of sitting up on a stage, facing a crowd of people, and talking about Daddy Joe sounded like a nightmare. I could barely think about him without starting to cry.

"I can't," I said. It had been ten months since his death, and while I was able to find comfort in all my sightings, I still didn't know if I could handle talking about him in front of a crowd, especially on the day after what would have been his ninety-ninth birthday.

"It's going to be nice. There'll be a video montage," my mom added.

"A video?" I whimpered. It was settled: I would be hiding in the crowd for this.

On October 12, 2012, my family convened in the lobby of the Javits Center, our lanyard passes around our necks. The crowd was intense, dotted with bright costumes and teeming with excitement. After heading down to the lower level, we found the windowless conference room filled with plastic folding chairs where the panel would be held. Snaking my way through the crowd, I found our reserved seats in the front row and placed my jean jacket on my lap, prepared to take cover if needed.

The panelists were cartoonist and caricaturist Angelo Torres, who had a regular slot in *MAD* magazine; writer and editor Paul Levitz, who served as president of DC Comics from 2002 to 2009; artist and writer Dave Gibbons, whose collaborations included the miniseries *Watchmen*; Daddy Joe's editor, Steve Saffel, from Titan Books; my uncle Jim, who co-authored *The Comic Book Makers* with Daddy Joe; and my cousin Emily. I held it together and even smiled at times. And then they announced the montage.

"We were lucky enough to have this video put together of Joe Simon," one of the panelists said toward the top of the hour. "Can someone dim the lights, please?"

"Fuck," I muttered under my breath. I looked desperately to my mom, who sat stoically to my left. I looked to my right at a young girl, a stranger—a fan wearing a black cape. Walking out at this point would be out of the question, so I slumped down and lifted the collar of my jean jacket to my mouth.

His face projected on the screen, and then his voice—that familiar sound, seeming to originate from the back of his throat rather than from a voice box. As he spoke, he pointed a paintbrush at the camera. His voice carried across the room and hit me hard. I lost it. The sobs rumbled from somewhere deep within, and despite my efforts to keep them inside—for my pride and also for my mom, who seemed to be refusing to look at me—they rolled silently out of my throat.

When I was in the hospital on the night Daddy Joe died, my dad was talking to my mom on the phone and looked at me. "Megan? She's okay," he said. "You know her. She's strong." Pride had washed over me for my dry eyes that night. And yet, here I was, almost a year later, sobbing like a hysterical child while my mom watched a video of her dead father silently, her face emotionless, strong. Disappointed with myself, I slumped lower and put the coat over my face, frantically drying my cheeks with my hand. I refused to resurface until I could emerge straight-faced like my mom.

When the memorial panel ended, the fan seated beside me in the black cape approached me. A cousin, after explaining that we were Daddy Joe's family, had let her take an extra seat in our row. My face was still wet with tears, and she hugged me tightly.

"You were lucky to have him," she said, black eyeliner smudging a bit above her left eye.

In her simple, kind gesture, I understood that he left behind more than his comic book characters. There was a whole world, a comic book universe, that had bloomed from his work, and with it, a community that would always keep his memory alive.

THIRTY

Life Goes On

2013

XX

Larry and I visited a few wedding venues before picking Fruitlands Museum in Harvard, Massachusetts. We looked at a contemporary museum with a nice outdoor patio, and farms with rustic barns, but the view from Fruitlands, beyond the charming rock wall, was what sold me. Sprawling green trees, and on a clear day—one we were lucky to have on our wedding day—you could see the top of Mount Monadnock in New Hampshire.

An actual wedding, one with a rented venue and a ceremony and a guest list of more than four, was a rarity for my family. I didn't grow up studying photos of my mother in a ruffled wedding gown and my dad in a sharp tuxedo. Rather, after their City Hall wedding, they headed to my dad's sister's loft apartment in SoHo for a party, where my mom wore a simple white sundress, embroidered with flowers.

Perhaps simple weddings were hereditary, like our autoimmune diseases. While Daddy Joe and Harriet's love had burned bright very quickly, instead of making their wedding a huge affair, they drove down to Elkton, Maryland, about fifty miles northeast of Baltimore. Right after the war, there were roadside stands with people officiating elopements—like Vegas, but without the drinking. They picked a minister off the side of the road and were married in his living room, where his wife played the clarinet.

When they returned to New York, Harriet's mother, Dinah, threw a fit. They quickly agreed to have another ceremony that included the whole family. Daddy Joe's parents drove down from Rochester, and everyone congregated on a Brooklyn street corner to watch them marry again.

Larry, on the other hand, only knew weddings with guest lists of around two hundred and realized quickly that we needed to find a happy medium—not only for the two of us but for our families as well. While his parents were ready to fund an epic wedding, inviting almost one hundred of their closest friends, my parents were terrified that I would make them walk down an aisle or dance in front of that many people. We were a people of intimacy, seclusion. Larry's family loved to socialize and be around as many people as possible.

Larry and I settled on a guest list of eighty-five people, which still felt huge to me but included all the loved people in our lives without overwhelming me. I found a satin J.Crew dress with a bateau neckline and seams running down the front, reminiscent of the 1920s. I loved the simplicity of the dress and how elegant it made me feel.

After signing the ketubah with our families gathered around us and a few friends serving as witnesses, we dispersed—Larry and everyone else down to an oak tree, and my parents and me to make a separate entrance. My dad drove my mom and me in their Volvo from the main house and down the dirt road to where Larry was waiting under the chuppah. I sat in the front seat of the car, wrestling open a can of Altoids, while my mom sat in the back in her blue, flowered sundress, chewing gum.

"Want to make a run for it?" she asked from the back seat.

I laughed. "Dad, pull a U-ey. Let's blow this joint."

We pulled up about fifty feet behind the seated guests, and with a nod from the venue event planner, we hooked arms. Larry's friend played Handel's "*Ombra Mai Fu*" on his guitar, a song from my dad's CD collection that I'd listened to over and over again as a child. We started from the large oak tree and walked slowly, me in between my parents, reining in my mom as she tried to speed up and get to her seat. I met Larry at the chuppah, our siblings standing on either side, and walked around him seven times to signify his being the center of my world. Larry walked around me seven times after, to fully break away the walls, and unite our souls.

Ombra mai fù, di vegetabile, cara ed amabile, soave più.

Never was a shade, of any plant, dearer and more lovely, or more sweet.

It was a beautiful September afternoon. The sun was starting to descend over the Nashoba Valley. Our chuppah was decorated with pink and white flowers.

"I want to take a moment to remember Megan's grandfather," the rabbi said.

Larry squeezed my hand.

"Daddy Joe and Megan were very close, and he would be thrilled about this marriage."

The sun warmed my cheek as our friends and family shaded their eyes with their wedding programs. I closed my eyes, not because of the glaring sun but for this moment of love and remembrance—the reminder of what was missing. They were just words, but they brought Daddy Joe to me. They allowed his spirit to sit in the front row with my parents, watching as Larry placed the ring on the tip of my finger. They allowed me to imagine him laughing and clapping after Larry smashed the glass and pulled me close for our first kiss as a married couple.

After the ceremony, we gathered under a large party tent, dancing, lifting one another up in chairs, a framed photo of Daddy Joe and me as a teenager propped on a table—my head resting against his chest, his arm around my shoulder. It was my first major life event without Daddy Joe—a day of joy while battling the sadness for the void of someone I'd loved and lost.

)(

When World War II ended, there was a housing shortage. Builders everywhere were scrambling to buy lots, build new homes, and take advantage of the high demand. At the time, Jack Kirby; his wife, Roz; and their three-year-old were living with Roz's family in Brooklyn. Daddy Joe and Harriet were newly married, living with Harriet's family in Brooklyn.

Harriet hated city life. She convinced not only Daddy Joe but also Jack and Roz as well to make the trek out to the suburbs. "The boys can work together in the good, clean air amid green grass and lush shrubbery," she said. They piled into Daddy Joe's 1941 red Buick convertible and drove around Connecticut and Long Island, looking for the perfect spot.

They ended up finding a brand-new housing development on a former potato farm in Mineola, Long Island. The small, cottage-like houses were on small plots of land—something like sixty feet by one hundred feet. They were the first ones there, so they picked houses right across the street from each other.

Although Daddy Joe and Jack were lucky to have work when they returned from the war, money was still tight. They didn't have pots and pans or furniture, so they slowly found the things they needed over the first few months, ordering the bare essentials from Macy's. But these household items weren't what mattered most. The important thing was that Harriet had gotten her house outside the city. It was time to start a family.

)(

One of my favorite books as a child was *Miss Suzy*, about a "little gray squirrel who lived all by herself in the tip, tip, top of a tall oak tree." The book sat on one of my paternal grandmother's many bookshelves on Long Island. Whenever we visited her, I studied the pages—Suzy sweeping her little house with a broom made of maple twigs, baking acorn bread, and falling asleep to the sway of her tree under the stars. The book helped me to realize something deep within me—the yearning for a place to call my own. I wanted my own little house at the top of a tree to clean and fill with smells of baked goods.

After Larry and I got married, I told him that I didn't want to get pregnant until we bought a house and moved out of our Brookline apartment.

"I want to give my child something different," I told him.

Over the next few months, we put in offers on seven houses and were quickly outbid. Walking around these houses, I ran my fingers over the wooden banisters and stopped to look out the windows to watch how the sunlight played in the trees and against the walls of the house. I fell in love with each one of them for different reasons: a built-in bench at the bottom of the stairs, a stained-glass window in the foyer, the attic space that would be perfect for an office to write in.

While at work, I found a new listing for a 1,900-square-foot pink house with three bedrooms, two and half bathrooms, and a decent-size plot of grass behind it. I forwarded the link to Larry with the message "Should we even bother?" It was starting to feel hopeless, and we were ready to continue our search elsewhere, farther out from the city and our jobs.

At the open house that weekend, I grumpily loved everything about it. "This screened-in porch is great, but what does it matter? The sunroom is perfect, but I guess for someone else!"

I asked the real estate agent if I could use the bathroom. "I have to test it out," I quipped. When I emerged from the small bathroom, which opened onto the kitchen (a turnoff for most of the other buyers), I declared, "Sold!" It was all a joke, because by that point, after having my heart broken seven times, I wasn't going to get attached again. But the original wood floors and large bright windows teased me.

While we stood in the backyard, a steep slope of ivy connecting the grass to the house, a family walked up the stone steps, their toddler declaring, "No, no, no!"

"Well, their kid hates it. Maybe we have a chance?" I asked Larry.

We put in our offer, the highest we could handle, and waited. There were multiple offers, we learned, and so we included a letter to the seller describing the joy we would bring to the house. The children, the cooking, the love. And then we prepared ourselves for disappointment again.

"Guess what?" Larry said when he called me the next afternoon at work.

"Stop it. I told you to only call me if we got the house."

"We got it."

It was as if fireworks were going off in my head. YOU. OWN. A. HOUSE. YOU'RE. GOING. TO. LIVE. IN. A. HOUSE.

X

The day after we signed the papers and were handed the keys, I drove over to the house after work. Larry would meet me there in an hour or so.

This is my house, this is my house, I silently repeated to myself as I walked up the concrete walkway and stone steps. It was summertime, and everything was in full bloom. I took the single key out of my purse, rubbing it between my thumb and index finger.

This is the key to my house.

I could see into the foyer through the sidelights, a word I'd just learned for the slivers of windows on either side of the maroon front door. It was empty inside, only bare wood floors ready for finishing and turquoise trim waiting to be painted.

But the key didn't work. As much as I jiggled, removed it, tried again, the lock wouldn't budge. I sat on the front step, defeated, and called Larry.

"I can't get into the house." I said, in a tone implying that the situation was to be expected. Of course I couldn't get into my new house. It was, after all, too good to be true. It was almost as if the universe realized its mistake and called a locksmith before I arrived. *Oh, her? No. She's not meant for a house.*

Larry wouldn't be there for another hour, but instead of waiting on the front step, I had a better idea. There was a stone path leading around the right side of the house to, if I remembered correctly, a few loose rocks, some large enough to help me get up and through the dining room window. I piled three rocks on top of one another, and while they wobbled a bit, I was able to get high enough to shimmy open the window. The window ledge was up to my chin, so in order for me to get up and over, it would take a good amount of arm strength, something I didn't have. But what I did have was the conviction that I would get in this damn house, because it was mine. While balancing on the wobbling rocks, I bent my knees and jumped just high enough to grab the window frame. Arms shaking, I slithered painfully over the ledge and landed, hands first, ass in the air, in my house.

✕

The previous owner, an elderly woman who taught piano lessons to local kids, had lived in the house alone for over a decade after her husband died and her son grew up and moved out. We learned a bit about her from our real estate agent, and from the house itself. In each room, the trim was painted either a bright turquoise or a deep pink, a nightmare to paint over. In the attic we found a green, scratchy rug from at least thirty years ago and an out-of-code low banister encircling the staircase. Wondering what was inside the hollow banister at the top of the attic stairs, we wiggled the top of it off, finding a cut heating pipe and a 1970s porn magazine, surely left behind by her son. Inside the dusty crawl space beneath the eaves, we found a few pairs of shoes and a single men's black dress shoe that had probably belonged to her husband. I loved finding old signs of life.

Along with the manuals for the stove and two ceiling fans, she left us the old yellowed blueprints for the garden.

"She worked out in that garden all day, every day," the real estate agent told us.

We studied the blueprints, noting what had survived from the original plan and what hadn't. The fruit trees behind the house were now replaced by a flowering tree we didn't know the name of and a small, spindly, wrinkled-looking tree. I walked around the yard, snapping photos of every plant and texting them to my aunts who lived upstate and had gardens of their own. *Hydrangeas, Japanese Maple, Dogwood, Liatris, Blue Grape Hyacinth.* The only plants I recognized were the conifers and roses that climbed the side of the house.

"This is intense," Larry said, looking over the plans with me. "But it will be fun to work in the garden." We both had fantasies of going rural and living off the land. Plus, we didn't have kids yet, so we had time for things like gardening.

Moving into a house was different than moving into an apartment. I had done that countless times in my twenties. New apartments were empty, wiped clean, sitting silently among dozens of other apartments that looked identical. They didn't show signs of life, except maybe a bottle or two of cleaner left under the sink. Moving into a house came with a sense of responsibility to continue its destiny. We were on a mission to continue bringing life into the old house.

☓

Larry and I moved on the hottest day of the year. We hadn't yet installed any AC units, so we opened all the windows and prayed for a breeze. I was thankful for the suburban air, which was unlike the city's, heavy with heat and stink.

There were other differences between the city and the suburbs—
beyond the yard and bigger rooms, there was less traffic and fewer
sirens. I saw the difference especially when it was raining. I could stand
at a window in my house and watch the rain appear from the highest
reaches of the sky, unlike when I was at my family's apartment, where
the only signs of rain had been the splatter on the metal fire escape and
maybe the sounds of water on concrete, if it was falling hard enough.
From my house, there was more than just the sound of rain—the way
it bounced off the stiff limbs of the conifers and how it gracefully
rolled off the red maple leaves.

I wanted the house desperately, but to actually walk through my
new front door every day felt ridiculous. I tried to shake the feeling of
becoming all that I hated as a teenager and young adult: wealthy, lucky.
Even well into my twenties, it was easy for me to use wealth in order
to judge someone's character—my jealousy leading me along like a
dangling carrot. I was so comfortable despising peers with money that
I feared any kind of luxury for myself. Our house, in a wealthy neighborhood outside of Boston, felt like wearing a stolen designer dress.
While I believed Larry deserved the house, having worked almost
twenty years at building his coffee and bagel cafés, I struggled to allow
myself this new reality. What had I done to deserve it? I thought of
younger me meeting present-day me and rolling her eyes. I thought of
Daddy Joe moving into his potato farm cottage, he and Harriet using
cheap paper shades from Macy's.

My dad brought up my copy of *Miss Suzy* during a visit. Looking
at the pages thirty years later brought back the familiar feelings, like
easing into a hot bath on a cold night. In the book, Miss Suzy is driven
out of her beloved tree house by six bad-news squirrels, but with the
help of some toy soldiers, she makes her way home. In the end, "The
wind blew gently and rocked the tree like a cradle. It was very peaceful,
and Miss Suzy was happy once more."

THIRTY-ONE

Finding the Tethers

2014

✕

I once read that red cardinals are loved ones who have died," I told Larry after we moved in. We were often visited by cardinals while sitting on our screened-in back porch. I learned how to decipher which one held a secret, watching for a certain knowing look in their eyes. It was usually the cardinals that perched closest to me, pausing for a solid minute before shooting back to the trees.

My life was split in two—before Daddy Joe died and after Daddy Joe died—and after moving into our house, I became acutely aware of how much my life had changed since we lost him. I was married, I owned a house, and soon, hopefully, I'd have a child. These were all wonderful things, but they created a distance from him. The more that changed, the more I was reminded how far away we were from each other.

Moving from an apartment to a house left us short on furniture, so the extra two bedrooms remained empty for a while, waiting to be furnished for guests, or maybe even a baby. It took Larry and me some time to decorate, and I knew that Daddy Joe needed to be felt throughout the house. The things I'd taken from Daddy Joe's apartment would keep him present in my own home for years to come.

In my office, a sunroom surrounded by windows, I framed a postcard that he'd sent me, displayed a cardboard cover mockup of his

memoir, and stored a box of smaller items—the flashlight, a lighter—
on a bookshelf. For Hanukkah the year before, my brother had printed
a large photo with Styrofoam backing of Daddy Joe and Harriet in
their bathing suits, back in their early days of dating. My brother had
quoted Daddy Joe underneath: "Harriet liked the tall guys." I leaned it
against the books in our living room built-ins.

In our dining room, propped besides the goldfish, was the framed
photo of Daddy Joe and me taken by the professional photographer
when I was a kid. It's a close-up, just our upper bodies, my arm hanging
around his shoulder, his glasses taking up 80 percent of his smiling
face, with the original sketch of Captain America photobombing us in
the background.

A plastic folder, the kind with the string closure, was filled with
photos of Harriet and a few of Daddy Joe and me strolling down
his popcorn-walled hallway, headed for the elevator. For years the
photos retained the smell of his apartment—cigar smoke with a hint
of old coffee grounds. In order to preserve that smell, I didn't dare
open the folder for more than a few seconds—one deep inhale was
all I allowed myself before quickly wrapping the string around the
tab to trap it once again. At first, that whiff brought me to tears,
transporting me back to his studio apartment in an instant. As time
passed, and the folder's scent reached its half-life, I relished it, closing
my eyes and remembering the days he was alive and smoking a cigar
in his chair.

I dreamed of Daddy Joe in the new house, the house I'd imagined
while riding the 1 or 9 train down to his apartment. The house that
reminded me of the large Long Island homes in which he had raised
his five children. The dreams were usually yellow—perhaps from the
constant cloud of cigar smoke—and they usually began with me sitting
alone in his bedroom, looking out a clouded window, only hinting at
the blinking skyline. The radiator, on which he used to try to grow
herbs and tomatoes, was there. The tall, overstuffed armoire that was

always cracked open stood in its assigned place beside the bed. Dreams where he himself appeared were few and far between.

After spending over thirty years in his apartment, every detail, every chip in the counter linoleum, every indestructible dust ball, was ingrained in my brain. I was grateful for the efficiency of memory and the magic of dreams.

Soon after moving, I dreamed that I was in Daddy Joe's apartment with Larry. Everything was sort of blurry, as most dreams are, but I could make out the warm yellow lighting and large windows looking out toward downtown Manhattan. We stood where his bed used to be, and as I looked at the window, Daddy Joe appeared—not clearly, of course. But I saw him. It was his pants (pulled up to his belly button), his belt, and his glasses that confirmed it.

"Do you see him?" I whispered excitedly to Larry. "I think I see him."

And then I woke up.

A few weeks after this dream, it was the Fourth of July. Facebook friends were posting the cover artwork of Captain America punching Hitler with the added text, "Happy 4th of July. Here is a picture of Captain America punching Hitler in the face." I shared it, smiling, thinking he would get a kick out of it. An hour later, Larry walked into the room holding a large, flat wrapped gift.

"Happy Fourth of July," he said, holding it out to me.

Having just shown him the image going around on Facebook, I joked, "What is it? A large picture of Captain America?"

I ripped away the paper and found just that. It was one of my grandfather's sketches that had been put up for auction. "You called for me, Mr. President?" Cap asks. If you looked closely, you could make out erased pencil lines around the lettering—ghostlike, reminding me of how Daddy Joe's hand once hovered over the page.

"I thought it belonged with you rather than with some stranger," Larry said.

"When did you buy this?" I asked him.

He thought for a moment. "I bought it about a month ago and had it framed two weeks ago."

Could my dream have been a heads-up from Daddy Joe that he was on his way?

I wiped a tear with the back of my hand and thanked Larry. "I think this is the best gift you ever got me."

We hung the sketch on our living room wall, where it caught sunlight from the east-facing windows, and where I could catch a glimpse of it every time I walked into our house.

THIRTY-TWO

A Great-Granddaughter

2014–2015

X

It must have been a Sunday morning, because I wasn't in a rush to get dressed and head out the door. Instead, I wore my house shirt—thin, long-sleeved, with a large Captain America shield on the front. I liked it because it was soft and reminded me of Daddy Joe, one of my many tethers to him. The house stood quiet, Larry probably out dealing with a bagel emergency.

My period was due that day, and although I had some familiar cramping, I took a pregnancy test from under the sink. We had started trying only a few weeks earlier, and I was constantly trying to push the enormous weight of what we were heading toward out of my mind. If I allowed myself to think about what a child meant—how our lives would change—stomach acid crawled up my throat. I wasn't ready to share my body with a new human, but I also knew that I never would be. I had to close my eyes and give myself over. Having lived in the house by ourselves for almost a year, it was time to give the house a new purpose.

After placing the pregnancy test on the sink, I walked upstairs, from our bedroom to the two guest rooms, one waiting to become a nursery. I stopped to look out each window toward the treetops full of summer foliage and birds. After a minute, I gave up my pacing and sat on the edge of the bathtub, then decided against that spot and moved to the closed toilet seat instead. Had it been two minutes? I looked anyway. One line. From somewhere unfamiliar, I was disappointed. Was it disappointment that I wasn't having a baby, or that my body had failed?

But then I saw a faint second line—so faint that I had to squint to get a better look. *Holy shit*. A warmth spread across my belly and into my chest. Our empty house filled with a new, somewhat terrifying energy. I instinctively held my lower abdomen. *Thank God you're here with me for this*, I thought as my hand rested against the large shield on my shirt.

X

The pregnancy nausea and exhaustion hit early. They sat on me, heavy, unrelenting and went beyond a queasiness that could be tempered by crackers. Phobic of vomiting, I lay in bed, motionless, meditating, praying to a higher power. Any movement or tiny moment of exertion inflamed the nausea, making me retreat back to the bedroom, covers pulled up to my chin, my eyes closed, praying again. Luckily, my boss allowed me to work from home for a few weeks, and I worked in bursts, until I had to close the laptop and return to my meditative position.

"I hate pregnancy," I whispered to Larry, my eyes closed. I felt guilty for saying those words. I was lucky to be pregnant, but the life had been sucked out of me.

At eight weeks, the midwife prescribed me Zofran so that I could stay hydrated and get myself to the office. I didn't love the idea of taking medication while pregnant, so I tried to hold off. On my first drive into Cambridge, a wave of nausea hit so hard that I had to pull off Storrow Drive, into the parking lot of a rundown hotel, open the car door, and prepare myself to vomit onto the concrete. I remembered the Zofran in my purse and decided that if it was prescribed, it was safe enough. I placed the tablet under my tongue and let it dissolve.

"Harriet loved being pregnant," Daddy Joe had once told me. I pictured her glowing, floating along happily and swollen with life. It was another thing that separated us, more of her genetics that didn't make it into my veins.

I thought a lot about genetics during the pregnancy. When the obstetrician asked me if I was Jewish, I was taken aback. I thought of Daddy Joe and his aversion to religion. But I knew being Jewish was more than that—more than his affinity for chicken soup with farfel, more than my paternal grandmother's recipe for borscht with a dollop of sour cream on top. It was more than food, culture, or whether I prayed. It was in my blood.

But then there was my paternal grandfather, Edward Countey, whose family had come to the United States from Ireland, long before the turn of the century. I thought of myself as a diluted Jew, sure that my grandfather's Irish blood would keep me safe from any possible genetic diseases.

Daddy Joe talked a lot about how I was part Irish. Talking to a stranger on the street who had just complimented my blue eyes, he would nod and say, "It's the Irish in her." He was disappointed in this fact, or maybe that my dad futzed with our lineage. But my paternal grandmother was Jewish as well, raised in Brooklyn by Polish Jews who lost family in a massacre outside of Lomza, Poland. She hated religion, too, and named my dad Christopher, maybe to spite Judaism, or maybe to please her Irish husband.

I had to wait two weeks for the results of the baby's genetic testing, and if there were any positives, the genetic counselor would talk me through the next steps. I was at ease, knowing I had this Irish card in my back pocket. So when she called two weeks later to tell me in a

soft, apologetic voice that I was a carrier for Gaucher disease, I wondered if there had been a mistake.

"I'm sorry. But this is only a concern if your husband tests positive
for Gaucher disease as well. And the odds of that are very slim."

While we waited for Larry's results, I kept thinking about the blood
running through my veins and the building blocks that made me, invisible but controlling so much.

Larry's results came back negative for everything. "I guess I'm more
of a Jew than you," I joked, relieved.

A month later, we found out we were having a girl.

"Payback's a bitch," my mom joked, remembering my teenage
years, then added, "Daddy Joe loved little girls."

Ж

I started maternity leave a week before my due date, thinking that I
could use the time to get the house in order and maybe get some rest
before all hell broke loose.

A small contraction woke me up the next day, April 15, at 4:00
AM. Remembering my midwife's advice, I tried to go back to sleep
and prepare myself for what would most likely be a long day. But
how could I go back to sleep knowing that labor had started? That
my whole life was going to change within a day or two? I tossed and
turned until seven before getting up.

Larry and I walked around the neighborhood, tried to take naps,
and soon found ourselves in the backyard, where we cleaned up wet
leaves, searching for buds of spring flowers. I didn't tell anyone in our
families about what was happening. I knew it was going to be a long
labor, and I didn't want to add to my anxiety with the hundreds of texts
that would most likely come my way. *How's it going? Anything yet?*

My mom texted me that afternoon: *It's Tax Day, don't go into
labor.*

I responded with a picture of an emerging purple crocus.

By the late afternoon, on a walk around the block, my contractions were strong enough to stop me in my tracks for those ten or so seconds.

"You okay?" Larry asked.

"It's getting intense," I said, breathing in and then exhaling after my stomach relaxed. But, naively, I felt powerful, almost primal. I was doing this. *I can handle this*, I thought.

By seven o'clock that night, as the contractions got more intense and I was hit with a wave of nausea reminiscent of my first sixteen weeks of pregnancy, I decided that I might not be able to do this.

"You're not far from the hospital, right?" my midwife asked. "Just come in and we'll check you and help with the nausea."

We drove the ten minutes to the hospital, me with my eyes closed, breathing through the contractions and now the urge to puke, and Larry stealing glances at me.

"One centimeter dilated," my midwife said, pulling the glove off her hand.

"That's it?" I cried from the hospital bed.

"You've got a long way to go. I suggest you head back home and get some rest."

We drove back to our house in silence. Although my nausea was now eased, I was annoyed with myself for having gone to the hospital before I needed to.

"How am I supposed to get rest?" I asked Larry, deflated, as we walked back into the house.

"Just lie down in bed and close your eyes. Try to relax."

I burrowed under the blankets and closed my eyes. But within minutes, the contractions began to intensify. I tried lying on my right side. I switched to the left. Soon the pain was so deep, so radiating, that there wasn't a position that helped. I tried a warm shower, letting the water beat against my lower back, praying for relief. I sat on the toilet, clawing at the windowsill, staring up at the dark, starry sky where I sometimes watched hawks circle.

I called my midwife again.

"Come lie down," Larry insisted as I waited to be patched through to her.

"This is the only place that feels bearable," I said through my teeth, naked, my wet towel at my feet.

"Hi, Megan," my midwife cooed. "What's going on?"

"I can't take it anymore," I whimpered.

"Okay," she said breezily. "Come on back."

As it was now eleven o'clock at night, we entered through the ER. While answering the intake questions, I clenched the armrest of the wheelchair I sat in, hovering over the seat, trying to escape the pain. They wheeled me up to the maternity ward, where I pulled off my clothing and put on a hospital gown, stopping to groan through each contraction.

"Let's get you back on the bed so I can check your progress," my midwife said.

Before I could, I was hit with another contraction. All I could do was sadly sing, "No, no, no, no," while doubled over the side of the bed.

"Don't say 'no,' say 'yes,'" she said sweetly.

I fought the urge to tell her to shut the fuck up.

I spent the night unable to sleep, a large exercise ball between my legs in an attempt to get the baby to drop again—when labor began, she had decided to try to climb higher in my uterus. The epidural quickly faded, not taking hold, and I was given a cocktail of drugs to keep me comfortable.

At noon the next day, my midwife announced she was breaking my water and we were going to start pushing.

"Are you ready to meet your baby?" she asked after the warmth of amniotic fluid puddled around my bottom.

"No," I said.

"No?" She laughed.

It was all too big. I hadn't slept in twenty-four hours.

"I need to do this in small steps. I'm just going to focus on pushing."

She nodded. "Okay. Let's start pushing."

It seemed my uterus could sense my trepidation, and the contractions started to slow. The next three hours were a blur. I was given Pitocin to invigorate my uterus, and the fetal monitoring strap around my belly was constantly being shifted to find her heartbeat. I kept my eyes closed most of the time, breathing when told, pushing when told, feeling the soft touch of an oxygen mask placed over my mouth and nose. Larry later told me that he could see every vein in my chest, that I turned purple with every push.

I heard my midwife step away and use the phone in the corner of the room, heard the words "trauma team" and "heart rate." *Me or the baby?*

There came the sounds of equipment being wheeled into the room, breaking the protective layer of what felt like our own universe with our single mission. I listened for the baby's heartbeat from the monitor through the noise of the bustle of our new visitors. I held my breath, ignored the beating of my own heart to listen for hers.

And there it was, that *thudunk thudunk* from deep within me, beating in the right time and rhythm.

"Well, never mind!" my midwife said, and laughed. "We're back in business."

※

The human that I had grown and carried for nine months was undoubtedly mine. When Lila flopped onto the delivery table, thirty-six hours after that first early-morning contraction, and after three hours of pushing, I cried with relief. But I also cried because of the energy shift in the hospital room—the space that we now claimed together. The midwife, also Jewish, said the *shehecheyanu*, a prayer to celebrate new beginnings. Larry stood beside her, joining in on the prayer, the three of them having a moment over my battered lower half. I was somewhere else. I thought of our house with its bright rooms. I thought about the life that I would give to my daughter. I thought about the man she would never meet.

After she was checked over and wiped down, my daughter was placed on my chest. While tracing my finger up and down her small arms, I thought about genetics again—how she had bits and pieces of all our ancestors, Daddy Joe somewhere in that mix, buried within her DNA. I prayed that his laugh, his love of eating, his artistic talent, that at least one of these things, had found its way to Lila. I gave her the middle name Harriet, a name that carried the memory of a great love.

After the three of us were moved to a private room, Lila swaddled and sleeping in a clear bassinet on wheels, I watched her—this new tether to Daddy Joe—from the hospital bed. Larry was sleeping with his back to me on the room's squeaky couch. I closed my eyes, drifting in and out of sleep.

꙳

Four months later, we gathered in the backyard with our families and the rabbi from our wedding. Lila's naming ceremony would welcome her into the Jewish faith and give her a Hebrew name.

When we first met with the rabbi to discuss the details of the day, he asked me why I wanted to name Lila after Daddy Joe. He didn't want the obvious answer, "Because I loved him." He wanted to know *why* I loved Daddy Joe. What were the characteristics that I hoped to pass on to her?

"His humor," I said first. "His artistic talent."

I had never put these feelings into words before. Those who knew me knew my love for Daddy Joe—it was an unspoken understanding. How would I translate that love into basic characteristics?

I looked at Larry, trying not to get emotional.

"What else?" the rabbi pressed.

I thought for a moment, recalling how it felt to be in his presence, to walk through his door. "His warmth," I added.

"He was an important comforting presence for you, yes?"

"Yes. I want Lila to carry that warmth with her. I want her to be Yosefa."

THIRTY-THREE

Uptown

2015

✕

Lila was six months old when she first visited New York. Already wound up from the four-hour car ride with her screaming her tiny head off, the city buzzing in its usual way, I thought of my house and longed for its calm.

My mom's friend let us use her extra studio apartment in a building only a block away from my parents' place. We set up Lila's Pack 'n Play in a storage closet only a few feet from the bed, jimmying it between a wall and metal shelving unit that held rolls of toilet paper and bottles of cleaning spray. Our bags were tucked between the couch and windows that looked onto a narrow courtyard.

I dressed Lila in her bear bunting, brown with ears on the hood, and we headed out to see my parents. She watched the city with wide eyes from her stroller. Even with the noise and constant movement of the city, I could feel Daddy Joe's absence in the air. I wanted to leave New York like a snake leaving its skin.

"This is where I grew up," I told Lila.

It was October, and the radiators of my parents' building were already clanking out heat. My mom put down one of her multicolored quilts on the living room floor for Lila to belly surf on. My parents' large Maine coon cat circled her, sniffing, while I watched nervously.

Lakota was known to have a temper, and this was her first encounter with a baby.

"Please," I begged my mom. "Don't let her get so close to Lila. I don't trust her."

Lakota settled onto her cat tree and hissed.

"My Lakota would never hurt her!" my mom exclaimed. My dad rolled his eyes at me.

Being in the apartment, now as a mother, it looked different, smaller. Even with my frustration over the lack of space when I was a teenager, the apartment always had enormous energy. Perhaps the unrelenting frustration during those years gave it the fiery energy of the sun. The apartment was, of course, still 550 square feet, roughly twenty-four steps one way and twenty-four steps the other (if there weren't any walls to stop you). But with time, distance, and a house of my own, everything looked delicate—the two wooden steps leading down to the living room, the hallway to the bedroom with wrought-iron bars on one side and my parents' bikes on the wall. The apartment looked fragile, like it had aged.

Later, Larry and I took Lila for a walk to get some fresh air. We headed west toward Broadway, weaving her stroller around people, each storefront exhaling a new smell like small offerings. We went straight for Riverside Drive, heading for the edge of the island where the Hudson River swelled against concrete. Even with the noise of the West Side Highway, we could feel the world open up, the cold air brightening our lungs.

"This is really nice," Larry said, surprised by the drastic change of the city within only a few blocks.

"The Monument is just down there," I said, pointing south.

"Ah, the Monument. Where Mommy did bad things," he told Lila with a grin.

"Where Mommy escaped," I corrected. "I was a good kid."

A few minutes later, I paused at the curve of concrete walkway that led up to the white stone of the Monument.

"Do you mind if I go up there for a bit?" I asked. "I'll catch up with you?"

"Sure," he said, taking the stroller. "Just text me."

The Monument looked cleaner than I remembered, maybe because it was daylight, but the stone felt the same beneath me, cool and solid. I sat on the ledge of the small inlet just as I had when I was a teenager, when I waited for the wind from the Hudson to carry away my frustration. Now the wind simply moved the flags overhead, clanking against the metal pole, busy with their own work.

Children ran around the Monument, hopping on and off the curved bench. On the backside, parents chatted, leaning against the stone railing. They stood where my friends and I used to squat behind one another to release a desperate pee, looking over our shoulders to make sure there weren't homeless men watching.

Although anxiety still hung over my head like a cloud when I visited the city, there was something missing. The two towers at the opposite end of Manhattan were only ghost buildings now. My teenage frustration and the biting need to find space had been relieved by my escape over ten years before. And the magic that had radiated from midtown had now evaporated.

With Daddy Joe gone, I was almost phobic of the city and the memories that its streets conjured up. What was left for me? Memories of teenage tantrums in my family's apartment? Walking home from the Monument at night, checking over my shoulder to make sure I wasn't being followed home? My refuge from all these things was gone, and in its place an emptiness where everything aimlessly swirled, looking for a place to land. Still, if I dug deep, I would find a love that couldn't be removed. I knew I would never move back to the city, but how could I truly hate the place that had once held Daddy Joe?

I met Larry and Lila back on Broadway. "Want to get a coffee?" I asked. "There's a good place on Columbus by my parents' apartment."

"I like New York," Larry said, as if reading my thoughts, my attempt to find any love left for the city. "But only for a few days at a time."

A block from the coffee shop, a man pushing a bike walked alongside us. Just another pedestrian in a crowd of many, a stream of diarrhea leaking from the leg of his spandex bike shorts. His steps metered, calm, keeping the half time of the rolling gears of his bike.

Larry and I looked at each other, his eyes wide.

"Fucking New York," I said, exhaling, exhausted, defeated.

THIRTY-FOUR

Shared Space

2015–2017

⋊⋉

Two birds were frantically chirping at each other on the tree branches above me. I was doing some writing on the back patio of our house, stopping to watch them flutter and spit at each other, bouncing from one branch to the next. I'd hung a small red barn from the cherry blossom tree that lurched over our pebbled back patio a few weeks before. I liked the idea of a lady bird stumbling across the empty, clean house and fluttering back to her mate to share the good news.

To my delight, the birds found the new construction, and soon there were twigs sticking out of its back door. I desperately wanted to peek in and see what was happening, but I didn't want to invade their privacy. As the taupe-feathered birds chirped in tongues at me, I tried to show my understanding by freezing in place.

"Don't worry about me," I said. "I get it. It's your place. All yours."

I'd been well-trained in respecting others' property. Once our apartment reached full capacity, I'd tried to limit any proof of my existence. If I broke a glass or left crumbs, or even a page of homework, on the dining room table, I was shunned and kicking myself for days after. I was a nuisance, not a daughter, which in turn had me baring my teeth at my parents like a rabid dog.

One afternoon, while watching a two-year-old Lila chomping on a graham cracker, my skin began to itch. "Oh, let's not get crumbs everywhere!" I sang. And then I cringed. I thought of my embarrassment when I caught my mom washing the apartment's bedroom door. Ro and I had been playing Barbies in my room, interrupted by the sounds of the sponge attacking the door.

I wanted to stop myself from becoming like my mom—the need for everything to be just right was hard to shut off. It was my *home*. But it was my daughter's home, too.

Just let her make a mess, I told myself, as she aggressively slid refrigerator magnets to the floor or when I picked forgotten stickers off the bottoms of my socks.

I struggled to keep this selfish urge to mark my territory in check. I was my mom, in more ways than one, but mostly in my need for control. My house was a precious thing.

Daddy Joe's apartment had a permanent layer of dust, no matter how often my mom came over to clean. The crumbs from his farfel, pretzels, and other midnight snacks lived within the lines of the parquet floor and attracted mice. He set up traps under the stove and under the raised white cabinets that held his VHS tape collection and three old printers. When he heard the squeaks of a victim, to the horror of my mom and me, he'd use a hammer to put the mouse out of its misery. But even with the mice and dust, Daddy Joe's apartment had offered me a sanctuary that I craved.

While I had struggled with the feeling of being a nuisance in my family's apartment, I wanted Lila to feel as peaceful as I had in Daddy Joe's apartment, cleanliness be damned. Buying our house, before she was born, and ensuring that she had nature outside her front door (not just rodents and pigeons) was my first step in giving her that peace. But most important was giving her the chance to claim her own space.

The rocking chair in Lila's bedroom, where I nursed her for hours, was soon replaced with a bean bag chair for bedtime stories. I imagined years into the future, the framed *Runaway Bunny* and *Madeline* illustrations on the walls stored in the basement and replaced with posters of her choosing. The four walls of her bedroom belonged to her. When she hit her teen years, she could sit in there for hours on end—sometimes in silence with a book, sometimes with a friend, and sometimes with music blaring.

But a bedroom wasn't enough. I wanted to prove my devotion tenfold, so I ordered a cedar playhouse for the backyard.

"Is this for you or Lila?" Larry asked, laughing. Even though I ordered the cedar playhouse for my daughter, it was no secret that a childhood dream had come true.

"Both of us," I replied, unamused, tracking the shipment of the house every day until it arrived. A week later, my dream playhouse sat on the doorstep of my real dream house—it was a nesting doll of abodes.

Larry spent three hours putting it together in the backyard, under a large conifer with branches hanging over the small roof. I watched eagerly from the living room window, thinking about how different Lila's childhood was from mine. It was the simple things that made her everyday life beautiful—the abundance of light, breezes that weren't weighed down by heavy city smells, and the rich, brown earth getting stuck beneath her nails. On walks, she held up acorns toward the trees, an offering to the squirrels who already cracked them open and dropped them to the ground. It reminded me of playing behind my friend Anna's building as a child. She climbed the metal bars secured in concrete, and I cracked open acorns, grinded them down with a rock, and pretended to bake acorn bread in my little treetop house.

After squeezing myself on hands and knees through the narrow doorway of the playhouse, I knelt, eye level with Lila. I asked her how wonderful it was. She moved from the stove to the side window, unsure of where to begin. Much like the storage area under the bed that sat in my family's living room, the house satisfied a craving deep within me. A lawn mower growled in the distance, the spring air car-rying smells of cut grass. A cardinal watched us from the dogwood tree across the lawn. Sitting back on my heels, I took in a deep breath, enjoying the seemingly impermeable space that I now shared with my daughter.

THIRTY-FIVE

Coat of Arms

2017

Ж

Lila was a late walker, so watching her run down a hill one after-noon at the park, grasping Larry's hand, I was full of pride. I loved her bravery. The sun was low enough to glow gold. Older kids ran down the mini-mountain without their parents, allowing their bodies to lose all control until they stumbled and fell roughly into the dirt.

Lila watched them from the bottom after her first foray, in awe of their muddy knees. It was an impressive feat they were performing, but as they barreled toward her small body, I cringed. I knew that she was invisible to these older kids. They couldn't see her wide eyes and grin.

"Again?" Larry asked, offering his hand to her. She nodded, her eyes never leaving the older boys, who were now on another run. She climbed with great difficulty, her small legs straining to carry her body up to the top. Larry pulled her slightly but allowed the majority of her weight to stay with her. She was almost three now, and needed to learn to carry the weight of things—her body, the world.

As they built up speed, the boys emerged from over the top of the hill, splitting apart to get around them. And as if in slow motion, the haze from the lowering sun behind them, I saw one of them was wearing a Captain America shirt. The shield, bold and proud, whizzed around Lila. She was clueless, but I silently prayed that one day she would catch glimpses of these signs. I prayed that I never stopped finding comfort in them.

X

With the growing distance of Daddy Joe's passing, Captain America offered a needed solace. In 2005, Daddy Joe told the *Philadelphia Daily News* that Captain America was always with him, "a guardian angel hanging over me my whole life."

The sketch that Daddy Joe gave to Martin Goodman is one of my favorite pieces—a simple sketch of Captain America with one hand raised and the other holding a shield decorated with stars and stripes. Underneath is Daddy Joe's writing: "Martin, Here's the character. I think he should have a kid buddy or he'll be talking to himself all the time. I'm working up script. Send schedule. Regards, Joe."

I imagined him bringing pen to paper and writing this note, unknowing of what that simple sketch would become over the next seventy or so years. What it would mean not only to the world, but to our family—a coat of arms, of sorts. Our family carried the shield everywhere we went. It was invisible to others, but it kept us connected to him. It was a way to share him with future generations—to remind us of who we were.

I started buying Lila an array of Captain America items: a small figurine, a winter hat, and T-shirts. These were things that could serve as her own personal talismans. One of her favorites was a Captain America coloring book. When she was three, her small hand held a red crayon in an awkward fist. She moved it messily over the lines of the pictures.

"Oops, I didn't stay in the lines," she said sheepishly.

"That's okay. You don't have to stay in the lines," I assured her, rubbing her back.

I stood beside her just as I had with Daddy Joe. All at once, I was eight years old again, standing next to his drawing table, the wheels of his chair rolling noisily over the divots in the parquet floor as he turned to grab a new pen.

This shield is yours, I wanted to tell her. *He is yours*. Instead, I ran my hand through her curls and told her, "Daddy Joe would love this."

We taped the picture to the wall of her bedroom, so she could see him every night before bed and every morning when she woke.

THIRTY-SIX

A Reincarnation

2018

)(

When I tried to figure out the due date for my second, very new pregnancy, the online calculator landed on October 11. My second child would be born 105 years, maybe to the exact day, after Daddy Joe's birth. It was a sign, I was sure. Meant to be.

"It's a boy," my mom predicted when I emailed her the results of the due date calculator. "Name him Josiah"—after Daddy Joe.

The nausea started early again, and so on Valentine's Day night, Larry and I stayed home. Lying in bed, I began to feel crampy. "Can you rub my lower back?" I asked him.

He obliged, leaving his side of the bed and walking over to me. "I don't want to do it too hard," he said, his thumbs pressing into the curve of my lower back. "I'm scared I'm going to abort the baby."

I laughed. The massage felt good, and I thought it was the end of just another annoying pregnancy symptom. We went to bed.

When I woke up the next morning and used the bathroom, I saw blood.

"There's blood," I whispered to Larry in the kitchen, where he was making his breakfast. Lila was focused on a coloring book. We hadn't told her anything yet, even though, in my excitement, I wanted to. Larry convinced me to wait until the twelve-week mark.

"Are you worried?" he asked.

"Not really." I shook my head, slightly nauseated by the smell of his eggs cooking. "I bled a little with Lila during the first trimester. It's probably the same thing."

But there hadn't been cramping with Lila, and the bleeding now was heavier. When the nurse asked me over the phone if it was like a period, I hesitated before telling her the truth. As if lying would keep it from meaning the worst.

"We'd like you to come in today and get blood work done," she told me.

"But I bled with my first. A little bit. Could it just be that?"

"I really can't say without testing your HCG level."

It sounded like she pitied me.

It was hard to comprehend the possibility that my body could fail at pregnancy. I was fertile like my mom, had gotten pregnant with one try. And on top of that, this baby was due on Daddy Joe's birthday. It seemed too cruel to have that gift taken away.

While a friend watched Lila, Larry drove me to the doctor's office. I was wearing a pad, willing it to be white every time I pulled down my pants to use the bathroom. I was disappointed each time, and as each hour passed, I started to doubt my body. By the time the phlebotomist asked for my full name before sticking the needle in my arm, I began to sob before even getting to my last name.

"I'm sorry," I said, embarrassed, my arm in the ready position, my elbow resting against the blue padded armrest.

"I'm so sorry," she said, squeezing my shoulder. The lab order in her hands and the addition of my tears made it clear what was happening.

On the way home, I told Larry to pull over at a small nature preserve off the highway. There was a river there, and as ice caps flowed downstream, fog settled heavily around the trees. We stood together, breathing in the cold air, watching a few swans paddle around a rock.

"I'm just going to walk out there." I pointed ahead, to where the wet ground met the water. I needed a moment to myself, to feel everything around me. In that moment I was hyperaware of my surroundings—the gray of the sky, the sound of the water, the bulky pad between my legs. I breathed in deeply and tried to prepare myself for a disappointing phone call from the nurse. But I still held some hope. Maybe she would call, laugh, and say, "Sometimes we see this in healthy pregnancies. Everything looks fine." Maybe, with Daddy Joe's magic, this baby would defy all odds.

I lay in bed for the remainder of the day with my cell phone nestled next to me. I figured if everything was still okay inside me, I should be horizontal to help things heal back up. But I didn't feel the energy and warmth in my uterus from the days before. My body felt eerily empty, like a spirit had departed.

At 5:30, the phone rang. I sat up before answering.

"Is this Megan?" the nurse asked. I tried to read the tone of her voice, but there was nothing.

"Yes," I said.

"Hi, Megan. I got your blood test results back, and unfortunately the HCG levels are too low for seven weeks of pregnancy."

This couldn't be real. My body couldn't really do this to me. This was something that happened to other people.

She went on to explain the next steps, what to look out for, when to come back for more blood work.

"I'm so sorry," she said before we hung up. I wondered how many of these phone calls she did in one week—how something so heartbreaking for me could be so run-of-the-mill for her.

I howled from the bed. I fought the urge to claw at my abdomen, devastated and angry with my body. This was something special, and I ruined it. I picked up the phone again and called my mom.

"Megan?" she answered. "Did you hear from the doctor?"

"I lost it. It's gone," I barely managed say.

We cried, both thinking of not only a failed pregnancy but also this lost tether to Daddy Joe. Despite my efforts to keep him present in my life, I wondered if it was all for nothing. Why hadn't he protected me?

I went through the following weeks subdued. The Captain America shirts did little to comfort me; they felt like a beesting. They had come to represent something magical for me, something deeply spiritual, but now, they were only reminders that Daddy Joe wasn't actually here.

✕

Lila first discovered the moon when she was about seventeen months old. First in her *Goodnight Moon* book, and later, when the days became shorter and cooler, she caught a glimpse of it from her bedroom window. "Moon," she said, her tiny finger pointing past the treetops and up at the bruised sky.

Every night, Lila and I walked hand in hand through her dark room, making sure not to trip over stray dolls and cars. As she got older, her observations became more detailed. After lifting the shade, she placed her hands on the sill and gazed up over the branches of the dogwood that grew in front of her window. If the sky wasn't cooperating, she rested her chin in her hands and groaned, "Oh, bummer, it's too cloudy!"

But on clear nights, she cheered and asked me to lift her up so she could stand on the sill, her body resting against mine.

"It's a beautiful, clear night," I told her one evening.

"So many stars. And blinks!" she exclaimed.

"Yes, blinks. Airplanes." I let her scan the sky for more planes while wrapping my arms around her. "You see those three stars all lined up?" I asked her, and sneaked a sniff of her freshly washed hair.

"Where?"

"Right there." I pointed. "That's called the Big Dipper. Or the Little Dipper. I'm not sure which one."

"Dipper?"

"Yes, dipper." I gave her little body a squeeze. "Okay, let's say good-night to the stars."

"Goodnight, stars. Goodnight, blinks. Goodnight, trees," she said.

"Don't forget the moon," I reminded her.

"Goodnight, moon."

I let her pull the shade back down, the planet stickers on her wall coming to life, glowing.

I was in middle school the first time I fell in love with the sky. The teachers led each class out to the front of the school building on East Ninety-Sixth Street. Though it was close to noon and there wasn't a cloud in the sky, the city seemed slightly shadowed, like a rainy day. We passed around special glasses and cardboard boxes fashioned to safely observe the solar eclipse, which was covering three quarters of the sun.

"Here we go! Any second now," our teacher announced.

Soon the city went dark. Not quite like nighttime, because you could still feel in your bones and the city's movement that it was daytime. I took off my paper glasses and watched the world around me. The shadowed stone buildings, the moving traffic, all existing despite the lull in light. I watched my teachers and classmates all standing silently, chins in the air. It was as though I had stopped time. I loved the partial stillness.

A few years later, my dad found me reading in our apartment's only bedroom. My brother hadn't yet been born, so the room was still mine.

"There's a harvest moon tonight," he said. "Want to go find it?"

We threw on our coats and headed out the front door of the building onto the street. The crosstown traffic was busy, moving loudly and swiftly. We didn't have to go far—the moon was sitting perfectly above the trees of Central Park and between the buildings of Columbus Avenue. It seemed impossible to look at something brighter than New York itself. Even with the squeaking brakes of the buses and the honking of impatient cabs, the large yellow moon subdued the city.

It's one thing to see a harvest moon or eclipse from the safety of the concrete sidewalks, the rest of the sky still dark and barely there. It's another to be outside the city, where the night sky looks endless, filled with glimmering stars. During family vacations in Maine or Vermont, after eating our dinner, my dad and I would go out to the grassy yard of our rental. If there wasn't a chair available, we'd simply lie on our backs, our feet crossed at the ankles.

My dad would start identifying the constellations and planets. "And there's the Milky Way." He'd point toward a white smudge running across the highest point of the night sky. That was when the enormity of the heavens seemed to fall against my body. The more I stared, the deeper my focus went and the more uncomfortable I became.

It was a fear not of extraterrestrial life but of the expanse of the sky—the fact that there weren't four walls keeping it neatly wrapped up in a box. When I thought about outer space and the dark forev- erness of it, I got that falling feeling in my chest, the same as when racing down the steep track of a roller coaster. When I imagined floating beside one of those massive planets, I was tempted to curl into the fetal position and protect myself from the unknown. How could anything exist and not be contained within something else? As a child, I was used to being contained in, almost swaddled by, the small apartment.

After Daddy Joe died, the sky became something different. I could look up and think of him. He was no longer in his studio apartment; the sky was his home now. Instead of city lights, his view consisted of constellations and galaxies. He always joked about going to the Great Art Department in the Sky. This made him godlike—easier to pray to when I needed him most.

Around the time Larry and I started trying for a second child, Lila began to confuse the character of Captain America with the human Daddy Joe. That year, when I asked her what she wanted to be for Halloween, she declared, "Daddy Joe!"

I laughed, imagining her in large glasses and trousers pulled up to her waist.

"I think you mean Captain America, right?"

"Yeah, Daddy Joe," she said, nodding all-knowingly.

"Well, Daddy Joe was my grandfather, your *great*-grandfather, and he *drew* Captain America."

She thought for a moment. "When will I get to meet him?"

"He lives in the sky now, so you won't get to. But we see him every time we see Captain America." I tried to keep it breezy, like he moved to Boca Raton and, unfortunately, we wouldn't be flying there.

Later that night, in her usual mission to delay our goodnight, she began her deeply profound questions from under the blankets: "What is the moon made out of? What is time? What's in the middle of earth?" And "What's after space?"

I tried not to think about the void that usually terrified me. "More space."

"That's where Daddy Joe lives?"

Sitting on the edge of her bed, I moved her curls between my fingers. The room was dark, only partially lit by the bathroom light in the hallway that she insisted we keep on. "Yes, he's in space."

"Just floating around all the planets? Like Mars and Jupiter?"

I pictured Daddy Joe sailing effortlessly through the darkness of space, an astronaut without any gear.

"Kind of." I stood up, brushing her bangs from her forehead, and gave her a kiss. "It's time for bed. I love you."

The truth was that Daddy Joe wasn't god. He couldn't control my life or the things that were happening to me. He wasn't all-powerful, and I felt guilty for expecting that of him. I imagined him up there, waving his hand at me and telling me he was tired, let him be. But it was hard to let him rest. How was I supposed to stop relying on him for the sense of calm and safety that he provided for thirty years?

That night, sitting at my desk, I studied the old ink bottle with

Daddy Joe's paintbrushes standing upright like flowers in a vase—sort of like a spirit tablet. It was my way of keeping him alive in my home, a physical place for him to stand guard. I took the brushes, with their splintered wood and yellow, dry bristles, out of the bottle. I rubbed my thumb against the years of paint layered on the handle, beautiful in a Monet-sky sort of way. I wondered if he had loved me as much as I loved him. He had been perfectly content living alone, enjoying his solitude—I, now an adult, craved the same thing. Had I annoyed him? Had my constant visits suffocated him?

But then I remembered his smile when I walked through the door. I heard his "Hi, Meggy!" when I called from a few blocks away. I heard happiness, an undercurrent of love. Perhaps my visits worked for both of us because we could exist in his apartment separately, and yet, together. We didn't expect anything from each other except maybe a decision on where we should order takeout.

Sometimes he wanted to show me his work—explain a new character idea, draft of a book, or re-creation. I obliged, of course, but felt out of my element. He was a giant in the comic book industry, and I was simply a girl who liked to rest under his wing. I struggled to think of something profound to say, but all I could do was nod and mutter, "Nice, really nice."

And maybe I was making this up for my own benefit, but I swore that when I kissed his cheek and said goodbye, I could sense a bit of sadness. I'd lean down to him in his brown chair, the morning sun making the apartment white, almost like heaven, me freshly showered and back in my clothes from the night before. He still hadn't brushed his teeth, his morning coffee breath thick.

"I'm gonna go," I'd say.

"Okay, baby." His hands would rest on each bare thigh, still in his boxer shorts.

I'd feel the stubble on his cheek as I kissed him.

"Do you need any money? Go in the file and grab some."

"I'm okay, I took some for a cab."

The cab ride was one of the many ways he spoiled me. Instead of taking the train, I could speed up Central Park West and be home in ten minutes.

"Okay, love you."

"Love you."

Out the door I'd go, the familiar clank of the door behind me and the rest of the world waiting outside.

 ⚓

A month after the miscarriage, I drove to my daughter's nursery school on a Thursday afternoon, music blasting from the radio. I noticed the beauty in the world around me—the green conifers, how the clouds puckered around the winter sun. It moved me to tears. All at once, while crying behind the steering wheel, the wind humming around my car, I realized that the miscarriage was like the paint on his old brushes sitting on my desk—just one of my many layers.

Perhaps Daddy Joe was still with me, allowing me to paint color after color, one on top of the other, to make something messy and beautiful.

THIRTY-SEVEN

Finding My Way Back

2019–

)(

I have no desire to visit his grave. His headstone, sitting beside Harriet's, right against a busy road in Farmingdale, Long Island, feels empty. Although it's where his body lies, I know that his spirit isn't there. There are only cars honking, the swoosh of them passing by, dirt, rock, bones.

There are times, usually on the anniversary of his death or his birthday, when I let myself fall into the depths of missing him. I let it weigh me down, sit inside me, while I beg the universe for a sign of him. The memories—the smells, shadows, and sounds—are comforting, heavy like a blanket. These memories enable me to go back to his apartment, where he became a part of me, like an extra heart. I fear there will come a day when I can't grab on to this memory, that I won't have the ability to fall into it, feel it in my chest with such an intensity that I'm short of breath. When I release the grief anchor and float back up to my current life, I inhale deeply. I'm ready to keep moving. I can only hope that he moves alongside me.

As the years passed, the anniversary of his death began to translate to an age that would never be—this year he would be 105! The world wasn't meant for him.

You're lucky that you got so much time with him. He lived a full life.

I've said these things to friends who have lost grandparents. But do these extra years equate to an easier loss? Each year you have with a loved one, your two souls are stitched together, tightly, until it's hard to tell where one soul begins and the other ends.

X

Eight years after his death, after grabbing a few things from his apartment, throwing them in my purse, and leaving his building for what I thought would be the last time, I came back. I was staying in a hotel only a few blocks away, which in itself was a huge step for me. I'd avoided the area on other trips, as if there was a force field around it. If I dared to break through it, I would be knocked down with sorrow, unable to breathe or even move. My mom went into the Whole Foods at Columbus Circle only a few times.

"How can you bear to do that?" I asked her.

"I can't go south of there," she said. "That's the farthest I can go."

I drove down from Boston with Larry, our two daughters in the back. Lila was four now, her new sister, Edie, only ten months old. After exiting the West Side Highway at Fifty-Sixth Street, we headed east to Seventh Avenue, where the hotel was.

"We're going to drive right by his building," I told Larry, clutching the steering wheel. "Lila, we're going to drive by Daddy Joe's building. Where he used to live."

Lila strained her neck to look out her window, to catch a glimpse of the brown-brick building with its wide face of windows. I glanced quickly as we drove by, but I knew I would have to walk over by myself—give him the respect he deserved.

On the last night of our trip, after Larry and I put the kids to bed, I bundled up and walked against the late November wind toward

Eighth Avenue. Some of the same businesses were still there—Patsy's Italian Restaurant and the McDonald's, now remodeled—but most of the storefronts had changed. Time had passed. As I got closer, noticing the slope of concrete at the edge of his building's front courtyard that I used to run up as a child, I felt the weight of his presence, like the childhood game: you're getting warmer, warmer, hotter, burning hot!

I stood in front of the automatic glass door, the doorman watching something on a computer monitor, and looked up to the sky. I breathed in deeply, inhaling the cold air, acclimating my body to this new altitude of grief. I dabbed at the corners of my eyes, catching the tears that began to fall, realizing this was one of the blessings that chaotic New York City offered: privacy even when surrounded by other people. There were too many sounds and movements for people to care about the red-eyed woman standing on the steps of this building.

I made my way through the door and approached the doorman. "This is a strange request," I started.

"Okay," he said, smiling.

"My grandfather used to live here, and I was hoping I could just go up to his floor for a few minutes."

He waved his hand at me, "Sure, no problem."

I relaxed. "Thank you."

"When did he live here?"

"He died in 2011. It's been a while. I haven't been in this neighborhood since then." I thought for a moment. "How long have you worked here?"

"Only two years."

"Do you know if any of the other guys are still around from that time?"

"Most of them are," he said. "What was your grandfather's name?"

"Joe Simon. He created Captain America."

"Yes!" He grinned, more energetic now. "They talk about him a lot!"

"That makes me so happy. Thank you for letting me do this." I looked toward the elevators. "Wish me luck."

"Good luck." He smiled kindly again.

I got in the elevator with a twentysomething girl. She pressed her floor—the sixth, Daddy Joe's floor. When the elevator door opened, she made a right, toward the end of the hall.

"Do you live here?" I asked.

"No, just here for a Friendsgiving."

She walked into 6L, the apartment directly across from Daddy Joe's. I waited for her to close the door behind her before I placed my hand against the cool metal of 6M. I was burning hot now, standing next to him, the energy, his spirit overwhelming.

I knew the apartment had been renovated and drastically changed after he died. But I pictured the apartment as I knew it. He was still in there, surrounded by his artwork, waiting for me in his brown leather chair. If I closed my eyes, I could still see every detail. I could still smell his cigar smoke, the mustiness of his shower.

I had thirty years to memorize every nook and cranny, every crack in the linoleum countertops and parquet floors. I could see his face, slurping a cup of coffee, and his old, spotted hands gracefully holding a colorfully battered paintbrush. When I let myself go back in time like this—to his apartment, to that feeling in my chest—I could find sorrow crawling up my throat as if I'd only just lost him. I was thankful for the clarity of my memories, regardless of that sorrow.

Across the hall, the Friendsgiving was in full swing, laughter and the clinking of silverware against dishes spilling into the hall. He would have loved having them as neighbors—their youth and energy.

It was hard to leave, but I didn't want to overstay my welcome or be caught standing alone in the hallway crying. *I have to go now*, I told him in my head. *But it was really good to see you.* My fingers fell from the cool metal of the door, and I made my way back to the elevators.

After thanking the doorman again, I stepped back out into the city.

Something had shifted. The city was now a living organism, evolving, growing. It was no longer full of grief, full of what I'd lost—Daddy Joe's neighborhood was no longer depleted. His spirit was nourishing the city, giving it roots. It was feeding the city as a body does the earth.

Acknowledgments

X

First and foremost, thank you to my agent, Rachel Sussman, for her dedication and humor throughout this long process. I'm also grateful for the enthusiasm and thoughtful work of my editor, Katie McGuire—your love of comic books was the cherry on top.

Thank you to those who offered their time and words of wisdom and support when needed: Rosemarie Buckley, Lauren DePino, Cameron Dezen Hammon, Eva Hagberg, Sean Howe, Erin Khar, Joselin Linder, Melody Malave, Deb Milstein, Melissa Stephenson, Nina Zoppi, and, of course, The Binders. Shout-out to my early beta-readers: Jessica Barnard, Matthew Somoroff, and Aimee Zoppi Confer. I'm lucky to have had Kathleen Schmidt and Carrie Howland's support and advice early on in this process. A big thank-you to Harry Mendryk for providing scans of my grandfather's artwork—you were a true friend to Daddy Joe, and I am eternally grateful for that.

To my grandmother Ellen, for reading me poetry from the time I was born and introducing me to the beauty of the written word.

To the amazing women Martha and Eva, who provided reliable and loving childcare so that I could squeeze in a few extra hours of writing.

To my parents, for powering through the pain of having a writer in the family. I'm grateful for your support and encouragement. Thank you for allowing me to explore whatever was happening inside of me and put it on the page. To Jedd and Jillian, for providing me with the cheerleading and words of wisdom that only siblings can offer. I'm lucky to have you two by my side.

This book would have been a lot harder to complete if it wasn't for my husband, Larry. Thank you for believing in me, for letting me cry, for lighting a fire under my ass when I was ready to give up, and for teaching me what can come of perseverance.